AF405281

Mosaic Hamsas
Original Designs and Various Techniques

Sigalit Eshet

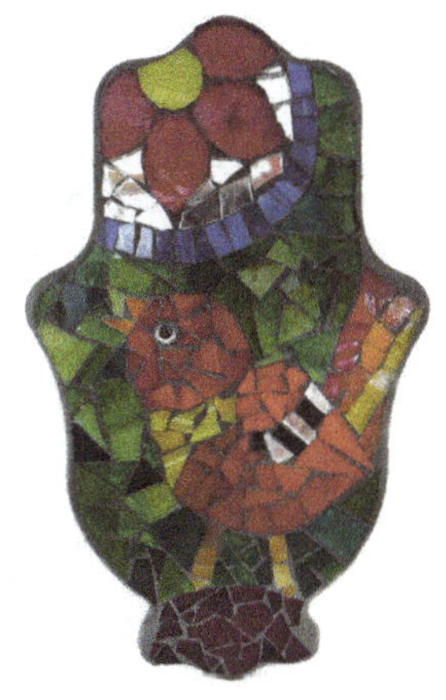

Copyright © Sigalit Eshet

All rights reserved.

First Print Edition: 2020

Photographs by Efrat Tenenbaum and Sigalit Eshet

Translation: AQ Group | https://www.aqenglish.com/

ISBN: 978-965-92788-7-9

www.sigalitart.net

All rights reserved. No part of this book, text, photographs or illustrations may be reproduced or transmitted in any form or by any means whether electronic, optical or mechanical (including photocopy, recording, Internet and e-mail). Commercial use of any kind of the content of this book is strictly prohibited without an authorization detailed in writing by the author.

Readers are permitted to reproduce any of the items/patterns in this book for their personal use. Any use of the items/patterns for commercial purpose is not permitted without a prior permission of the Author.

Thank you for respecting the hard work of this author.

Disclaimer

All do-it-yourself activities involve risk, and your safety is your own responsibility, including proper use of equipment and safety gear, and determining whether you have adequate skill and experience.

Some of the resources used for these projects are dangerous unless used properly and with adequate pre-cautions, including safety gear.

Some illustrative photos do not depict safety precautions or equipment, in order to show the project step more clearly.

Some projects are user-submitted, and appearance of a project in this format does not indicate it has been checked for safety or functionality. Use of the instructions and suggestions is at your own risk.

I disclaim all responsibility for any resulting damage, injury, or expense. It is your responsibility to make sure that your activities comply with all applicable laws.

Contents

Introduction

I've been creating mosaic hamsas for years now, utilizing a myriad of colors, shapes and sizes. I've found this motif to be quite popular and great housewarming gift for a loved one or just for sprucing your home with some good fortune. Moreover, the shape of the hamsa fascinates and challenges me – constantly reinventing a new design in this special design of the human palm. Since it creates an image, one can integrate different materials, use the hand itself as a basis or invent a more abstract design.

So, what's a Hamsa?

The hamsa decorated palm is a traditional good luck charm. Its shape is of an open palm with the fingers close together, meant to bring good fortune and ward off the evil eye. The word "hamsa" is Arabic for "five", after the charm's five fingers.

The hamsa's origins are ancient and are denoted in Judaism and Islam as well.

The Jewish hamsa points upward to the sky with a spiritual significance, while the Muslim one points downward to the ground, for good fortune and to ward off evil spirits from below.

The hamsa will usually be symmetric, with the thumb and pinkie identical and parallel.

In the past, it was the symbol of the moon goddess, and the downward version was also used as a protection amulet in battle for habitants of the Mediterranean, prior to the rise of monotheistic religions.

According to Islamic tradition, the hamsa symbolizes the birth of Fatma, daughter of prophet Mohammed. As the legend goes, she was making Hilbeh when her husband entered the room with another woman. She was so stricken that she dropped the spoon into the pot, and continued to stir with her bare palm. Fatma's hand became the symbol of tolerance and the power of faith. The tear she shed because of her husband is also seen on the hamsa's center, in the shape of an eye to protect against evil eye. The hamsa's five fingers also signify the five pillars of Islam: Profession of faith, prayer, almsgiving, fasting and pilgrimage.

In Jewish tradition, the hamsa represents the fifth letter of the Hebrew alphabet, which also symbolizes the Hebrew God, the shape of the fig leaf of the biblical Seven Species, the five senses and the five fifths of the Torah. It may have also signified an outstretched hand, a symbol of giving, candidness and a peaceful greeting.

Either way, the hamsa has decorated doorways, necks, wallets and keychains for many years. It has many motifs such as eyes, fish, the Star of David, blessings and prayers: For good luck, warding off the evil eye and for protection.

In this book, you'll find numerous examples of mosaic hamsa, crafted through various techniques. One can craft a wood-based mosaic hamsa for home decoration, hang it on a tile outdoors, or incorporate a blessing or poem with a special technique. You can also craft a hamsa following the cut, or trace it to a square or rectangle and add a background.

I'll also tell you of a special hamsa project I created for a school in order to bring together Jews and Arabs, and of another major project called Hamsa for Peace, in which I took part.

At the end of the book you'll find a link to a file containing all examples – have fun!

Personally, I prefer to craft my hamsas with the fingers pointing down, but I'll leave that to your own discretion.

I hope you enjoy crafting, and may your hamsas protect you and bring you good fortune!

Sigalit

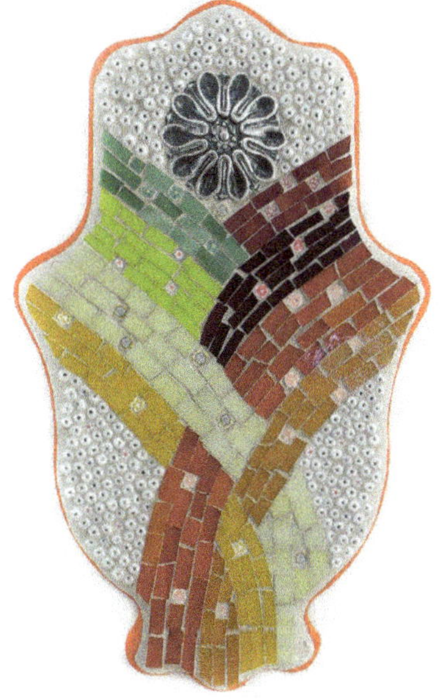

Cutting tools

There are various tools used for mosaic work, and it's recommended that you have at least the basic ones in your arsenal. Each material will have its own best-suited tool. Using the right tool can make the work tremendously easier and more accurate.

Since this book covers the use of various materials, I recommend that you own at least one of each tool shown here (at least for cutting glass and ceramics). Naturally, you can choose whichever material you desire for making the suggested examples.

Below are detailed instructions on work with each instrument.

Ceramic Cutting Tools

Mosaic tile cutter (red handle) – for cutting and grinding ceramic tiles. You can get these in hardware stores.

Compound Tile Nipper - for cutting and grinding ceramic tiles. This tool has Twice the power of conventional cutter. You can find it online or in specialized stores. I love using this tool, as it's strong and easy to cut with.

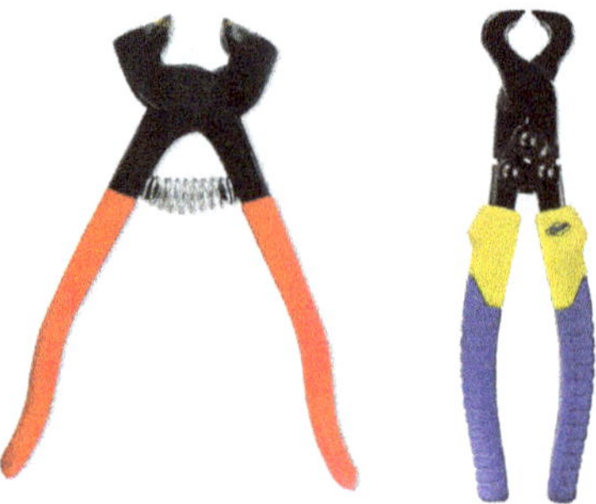

Ceramic cutting machine – For advanced cutters. Used to cut ceramic into straight and accurate tiles. I did not use the cutting machine for projects in this book.

Hammer – For cutting thick ceramic, or when you want to cut random shapes. Please note that when you cut ceramic with a hammer, you should wrap the ceramic with an old towel and place it on top of a thick wood or metal surface.

Glass Cutting Tools

Wheeled glass nipper – for cutting glass and plates.

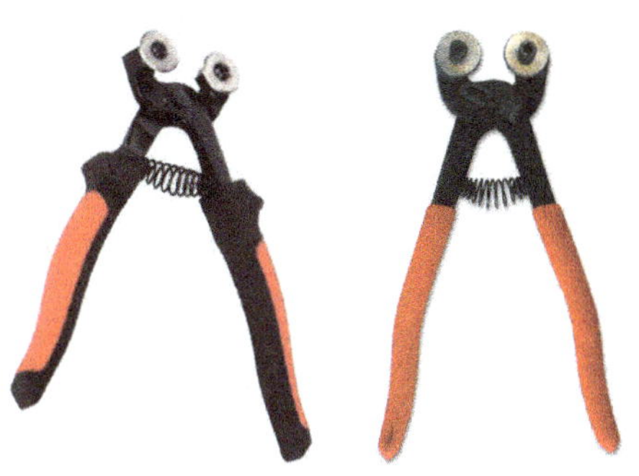

If you wish to integrate glass from a large panel into the mosaic, you'll need several other tools used for cutting glass (also used for making stained glass). I like using these panels for their shine and pleasing appearance, and since they come in a wide variety of colors.

Glass cutter – For cutting straight lines or specific shapes. There are several kinds of cutters. The difference is in shape and price. I recommend you to try out and decide which cutter works best for you. All cutters have a small wheel at the top, and the difference is mainly in the grip angle. For example:

Glass cutter with a straight handle

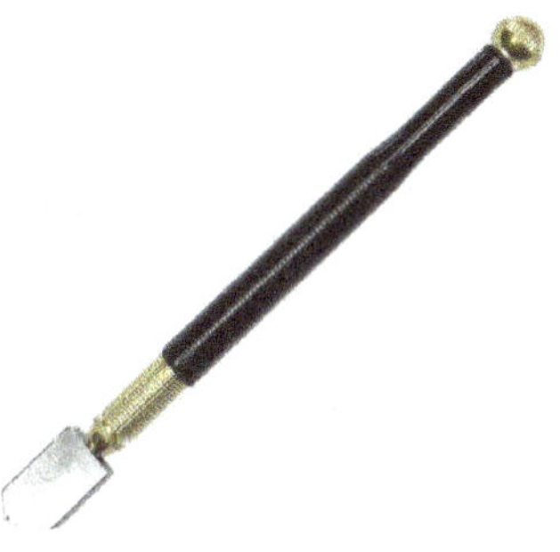

Glass cutter with plastic grip handle

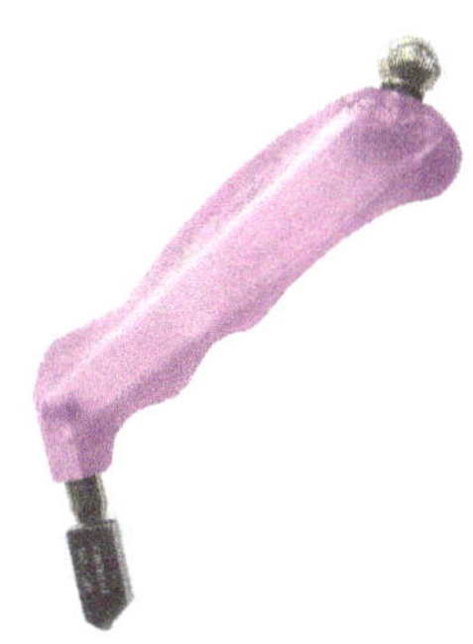

Pliers

Breaking glass plier/Running plier – For Breaking glass after marking it with the glass cutter.

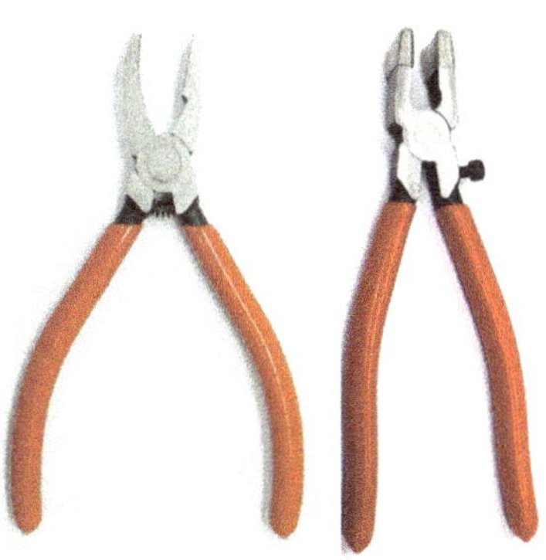

Grozer pliers - For breaking glass along score lines that can't be handled comfortably by hand. The cutter has two sides, one straight and the one curved.

Preparation tools

Pencil – For drawing the desired pattern on the substrate material.

Ruler – For marking straight lines.

T-Ruler – For guiding the glass cut into straight lines.

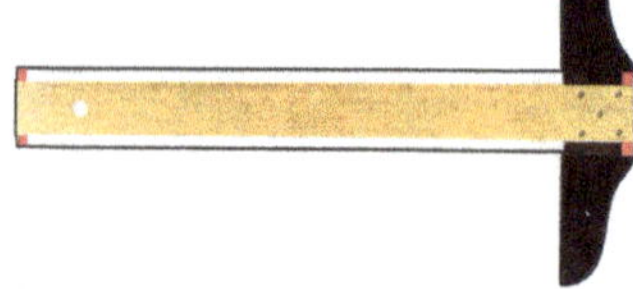

Glass paint marker – For marking shapes on
the glass. It's better to have one black and one white or gold, for dark glass panels.

Latex gloves – For protecting your hands against scratches and dirt.

Rubber gloves –Put these on before you start working **with grout.**

Plastic containers – For glue, water, cut glass or beads and mixing colors.

Small brush – For cleaning the surface from dust and small particles.

Thin flat screwdriver – For cleaning tile adhesive residue.

Tweezers – For placement of small parts.

Paintbrush – For adhesive application.

Wooden mixing sticks – For mixing grout and applying tile adhesive.

Carbon paper – To copy your design from paper onto your substrate material.

Safety Equipment

Safety goggles – For protecting your eyes against
ceramic fragments. Use it when cutting ceramic.

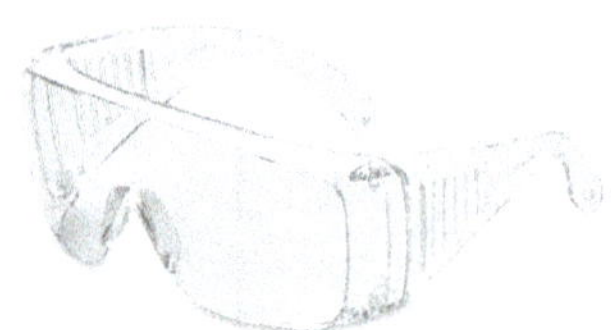

Dust mask – Use this when preparing the grout.

Safety Instructions

Safety is imperative when making mosaic. Glass and cut ceramic Have sharp edges and can shoot out toward you, so use caution.

1. Always wear closed shoes. Don't walk barefoot on the floor where you are working. Small fragments can be difficult to spot and remove.

2. Wear safety goggles and gloves when cutting glass plates.

3. Use a small brush to clean the working surface. Don't clean the small fragments with bare hands!

4. Vacuum the floor after finishing – it's better than just sweeping dust around.

5. Keep young children and pets away.

6. Keep some adhesive bandages handy.

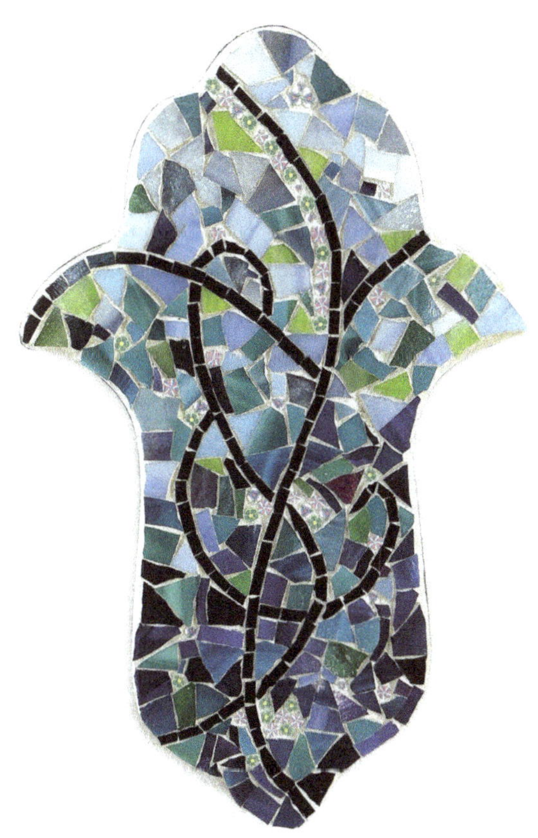

Materials

I like working with as many types of media, and mix various materials into the mosaic. This creates a more colourful and interesting piece. In this book, you'll find an assortment of pieces using diverse materials and their mixtures.

The Hamsa is actually a picture, so there's no need to maintain a uniform height for all pieces, and one can try different combinations of colors, texture, sizes and media.

In the list below, you'll find various materials which suit mosaic works, but naturally you can try and integrate any medium you see fit.

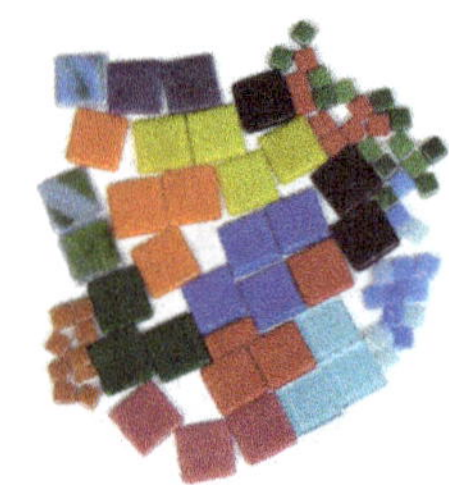

Colorful ceramic tiles – Can be found in a variety of shapes and sizes.

Glass tiles – These come in uniform size squares and in many colors. They have one smooth flat side (which should face up), and a rough side (to which glue is applied).

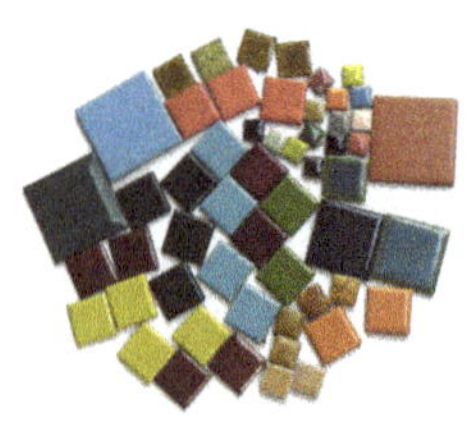

Stained glass – Can be found in many colors and textures. You can cut it with a nipper or a glass cutter.

Ceramic square tiles – These are available in many colors, textures, and shapes. They come mostly on a square mesh.

Vitreous glass mosaic tiles – Ready-made square glass tiles in a variety of sizes and colors. The glass can be glossy or grainy, clear or opaque, uniform or blended. Tile sizes start at 1 cm2/0.15in2, and you can buy sheets of sticker tiles or by weight.

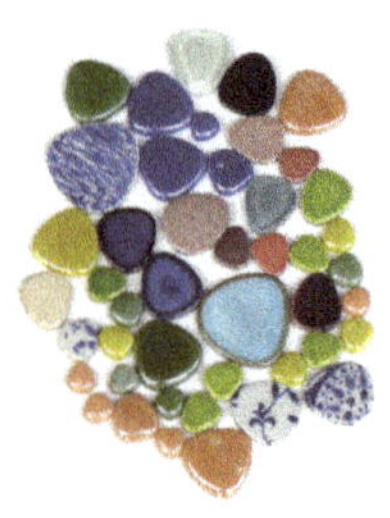

China and crockery – Using proper safety precautions, these can be broken or used to cut your own tiles from. Plates often have that unique texture that you can't find in tiles.

Found objects – These include seashells, glass beads, buttons, glass nuggets, necklaces, brooches, etc. Use it to decorate and enrich your work.

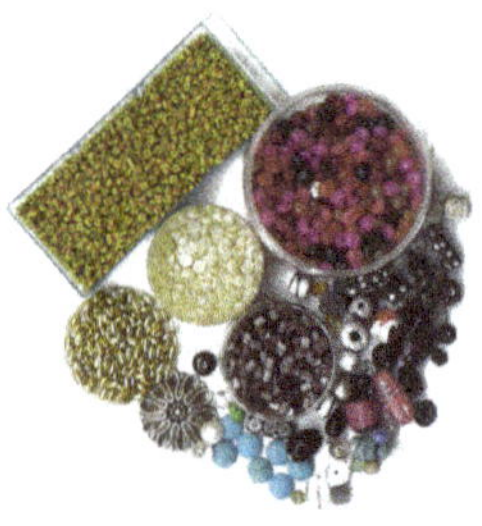

 Mirrors – These can add a beautiful reflective touch to any mosaic piece.

Polymer clay – Use polymer clay, like Fimo™, to decorate your mosaic work.

Beads – I like incorporating different types of beads into mosaics: Glass or plastic, round or square, tiny or large. Each necklace that falls out of my favor ends up in my bead box and quickly finds its way into a mosaic piece.

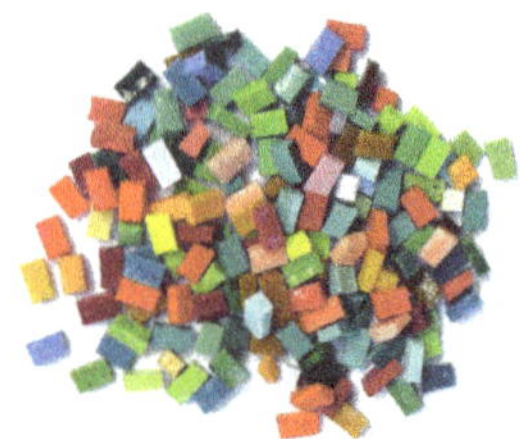

Smalti – Colored glass chunks with very vivid colors. We'll leave the Smalti to more advanced installments; the book will not cover this material.

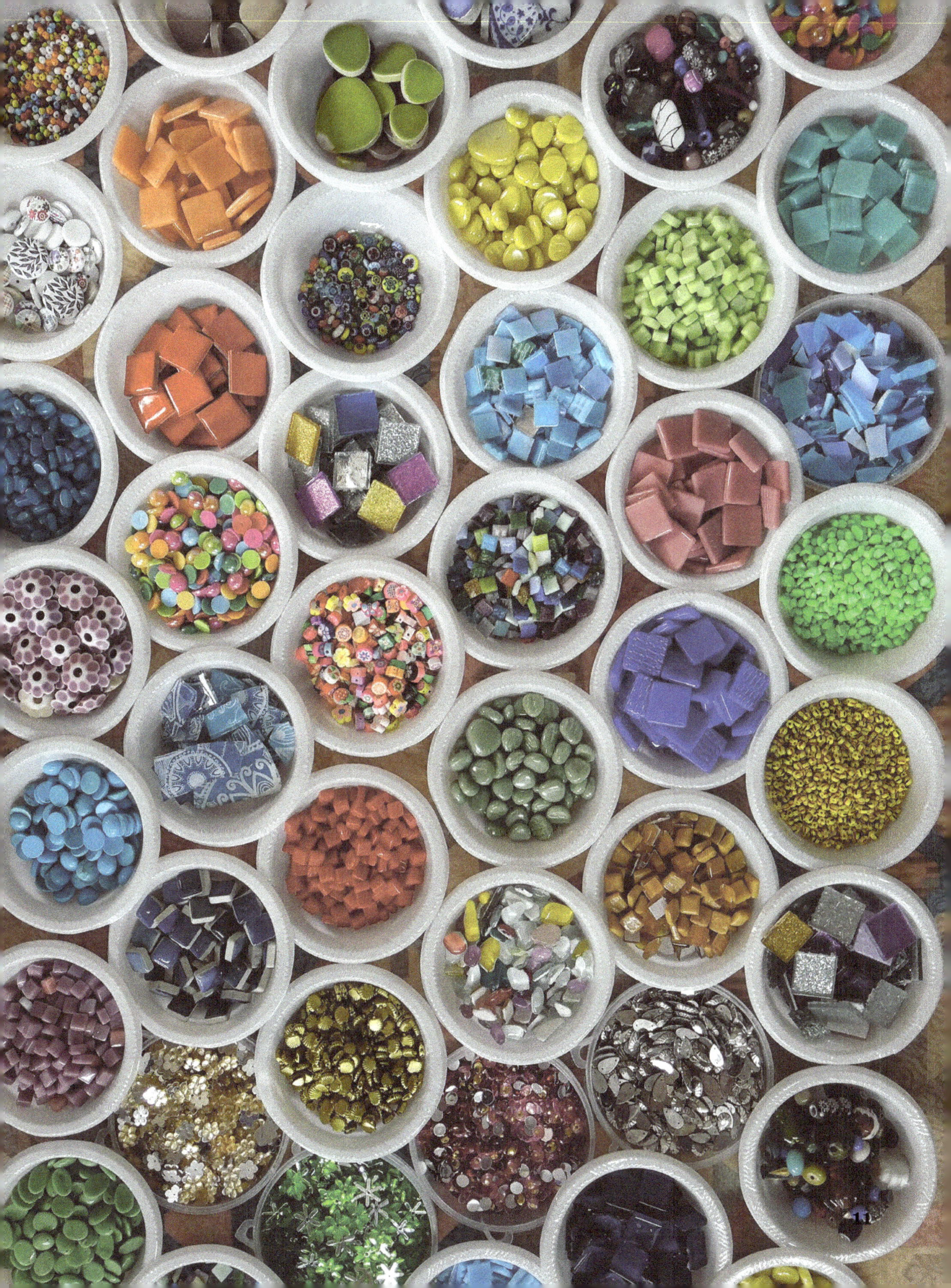

Adhesives

For proper use of glue, always read the manufacturer's instructions. Use the glue that is most comfortable for you to work with.

It is very important to adjust the glue to the platform on which you are working. On wooden bases we use white glue, which suits indoor works that will generally stay away from moisture and direct sunlight. When we use a metal base mosaic, we will use tile adhesive - this way the work can remain outside in all weather conditions without issue.

PVA white glue – This glue is useful for most mosaic works, especially wooden surfaces. I recommend first sampling on a small segment to verify its strength. There are various kinds of white glue, with varying levels of adhesiveness.

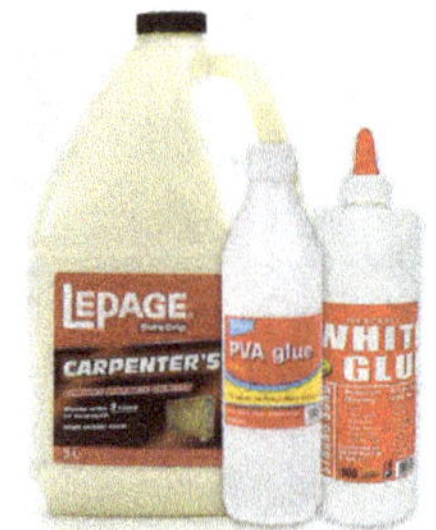

I prefer using reinforced white glue due to its rapid drying.

Mosaic tile adhesive – For sticking ceramic tiles onto metal, clay or for any outdoor work.

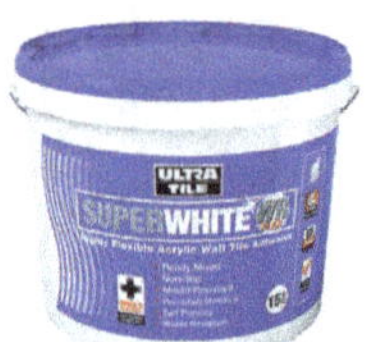
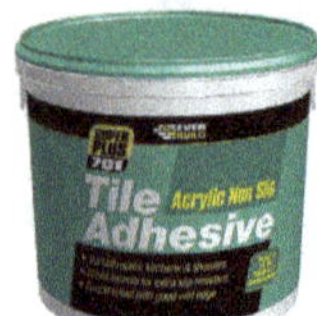

Glass glue – For sticking tiles onto a glass substrate (like E6000).

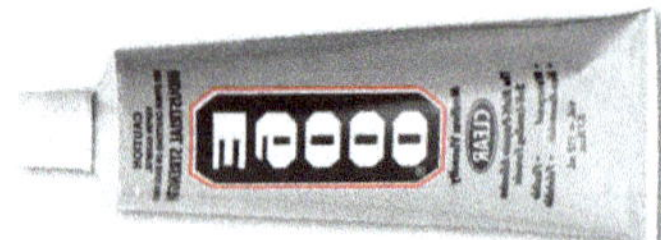

Grout

We use the grout for filling the gaps between tiles.

NOTE: There are different types of grout. Most of them come in powdered form, which you will need to mix with water according manufacturer instructions. Grout also comes in different colors, so choose the right color for your work. You can also mix acrylic paint into white grout to make your own custom colored grout, but if you do this, be sure that the final work is not exposed to sunlight or moisture.

Working with grout can be messy, so wear appropriate clothing and wear gloves before you begin.

Water – For preparing grout and cleaning.

Small squeegee – For gripping and applying the grout to straight surfaces.

Sponge or cotton rags – For grout cleaning.

Old newspapers – For placing under your work to maintain a clean work surface.

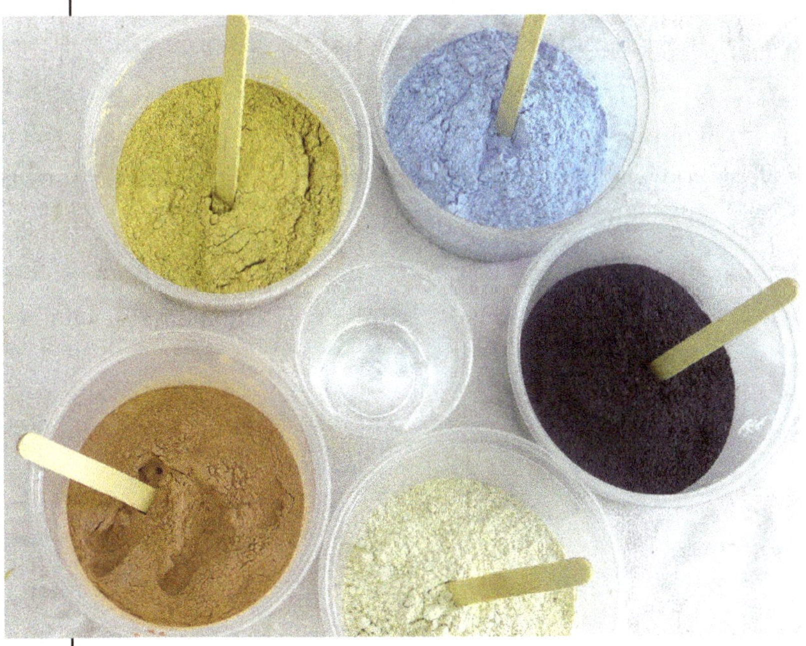

Choosing the Right Color Grout

The color of grout you select will significantly influence the final look. In fact, if you create the exact same piece twice with different grout finishes, the mosaic will look utterly different.

When choosing the grout color, ask yourselves what you want to emphasize – the shape or the background? Perhaps the harmony of the mosaic?

A few tips to help you choose the most appropriate color:

1. If your mosaic has a main subject and a background, make sure the background blends in and does not contest the subject. Figure out which color can highlight the main image, should it be light or dark, and what will its effect on the subject be.

2. If you're not sure about the right color of grout – gray seems to always get the job done. It's a neutral color suitable for most pieces. Remember that the final work will have a lighter shade than when it's wet during processing.

3. For pieces with colored glass should be complemented with dark grout, as it emphasizes and intensifies the glass' colors.

4. Sometimes it's best to treat grout as an additional color in the work, which gives it more depth. Here, you should use colored grout to blend in the mosaic without taking over.

5. Try to avoid using white grout – it highlights blemishes in the work. Use it when you wish to accentuate the white look or when the mosaic is glued tightly on a white background.

6. You can pour a little grout powder into the crack between the tesserae in one of the piece's corners to test and see which color you get.

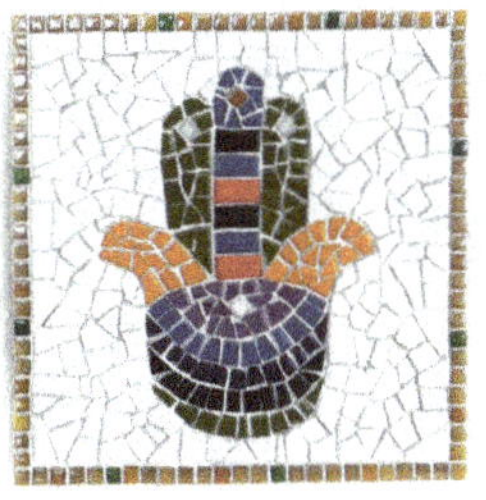

Project No. 1: Hot Pot Coaster

A hot pot coaster or a picture? Why not both?

Here's how to create a mosaic that doubles as a coaster and a wall ornament.

One of the most popular pieces in the mosaic workshops I deliver is a pot coaster – a product which sits well on any dinner table, is practical and can be given as a personal gift. If we add a hanger on the back, it can decorate a wall with just as much grace.

Materials:

Wood base size 9.5"x9.5"/24x24 cm
Mosaic tiles (I used 2.5x2.5cm/1" squares): green, 2 shades of blue, purple, orange, red
White tiles for background
Small orange and green squares for the frame + 3 white squares

PVA white glue
Paintbrush
Tile cutter
Gray Grout
Grout Gear: Mixing bowl, water, a wooden stick, rags, gloves

1 Trace the pattern to the wooden surface with a pencil and tracing paper.

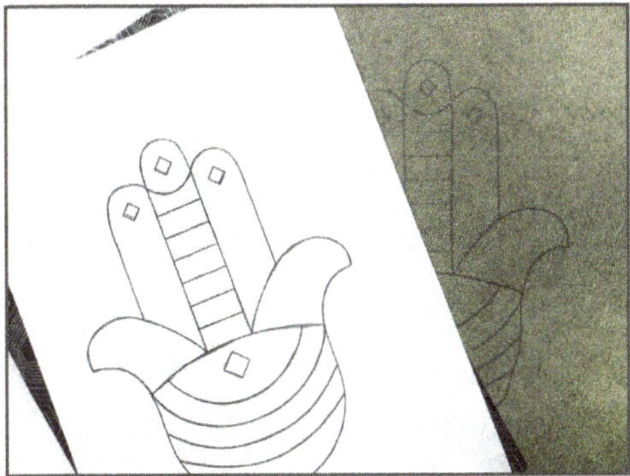

2 Start with the center eye: Glue a small white square in the middle of the hamsa. Using the pliers, cut a piece of purple tile to small shapes and glue around the white square (see pliers use instructions below).

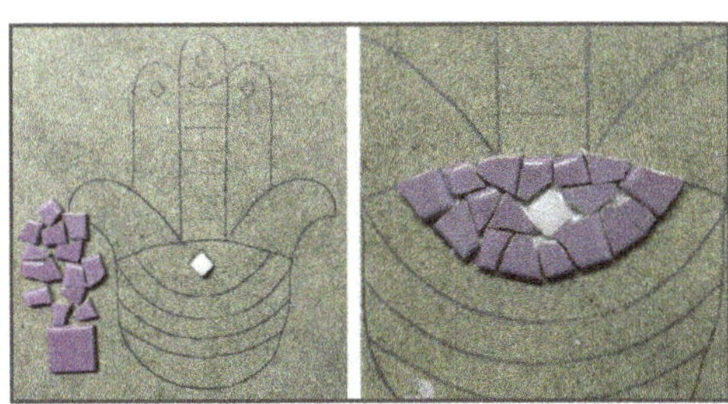

3 For the blue arch, it's better to use 2.5" ceramic tiles. Split each one in two with a straight cut, and split each half in three with a diagonal cut as seen in the photo.

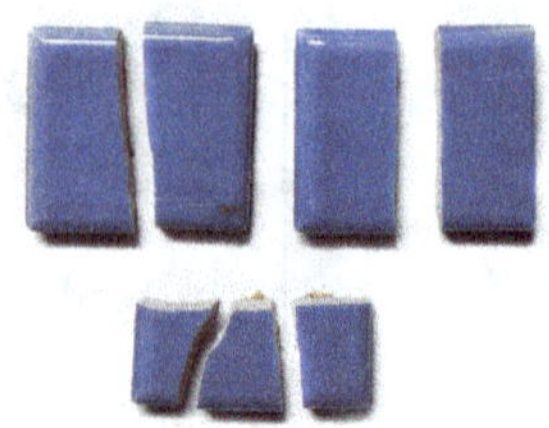

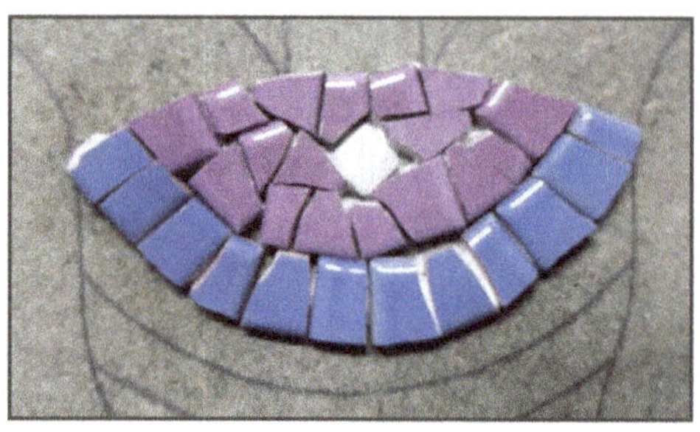

4 Paste the blue pieces onto the arch. Align the bottom part and use the diagonal pieces to create an aesthetic arch.

5 Use the same method to create the dark blue arch and add triangles at the edges.

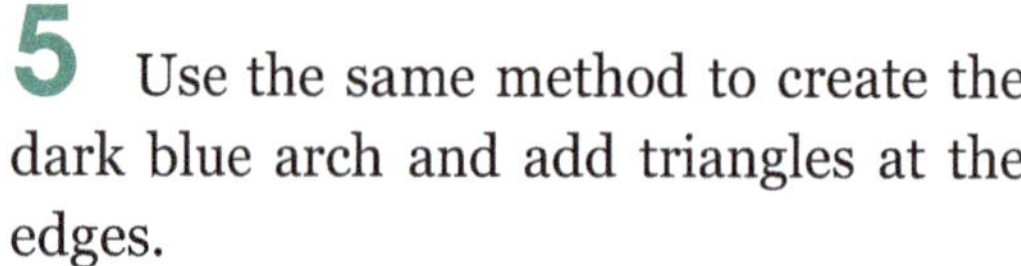

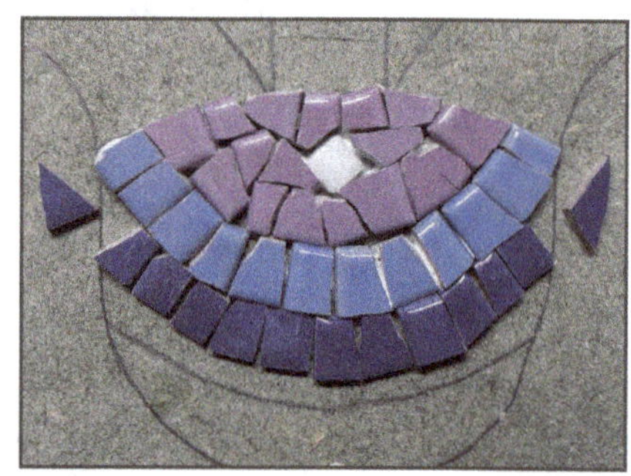

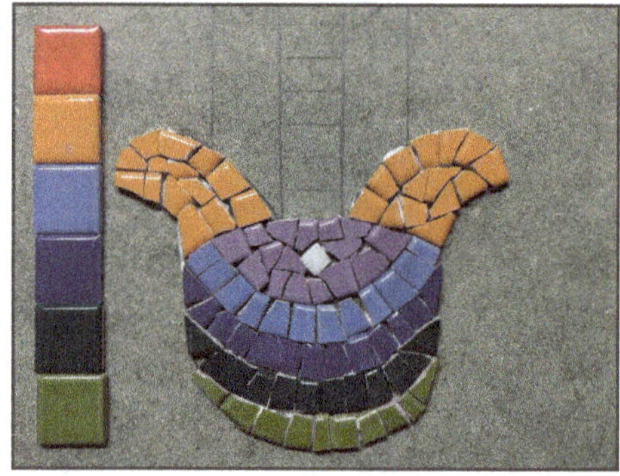

6 Thus, paste two additional arches in two shades of green. On the bottom arch, maintain a nice, round shape. Cut small pieces of orange tile and glue them on the two fingers pointing outward.

7 The hamsa's middle finger will be composed of red, blue and green half-squares. Paste two additional white squares at the top of the two remaining fingers, and an orange square at the top of the middle fingers, and proceed to paste small blue pieces around that.

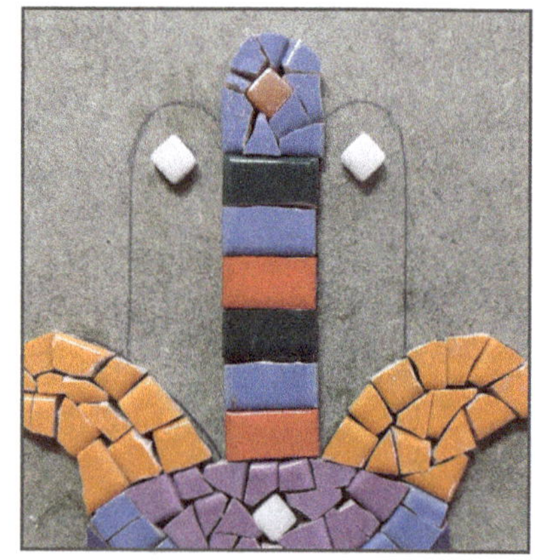

8   In the two remaining fingers, paste the green tiles you've cut into small pieces.

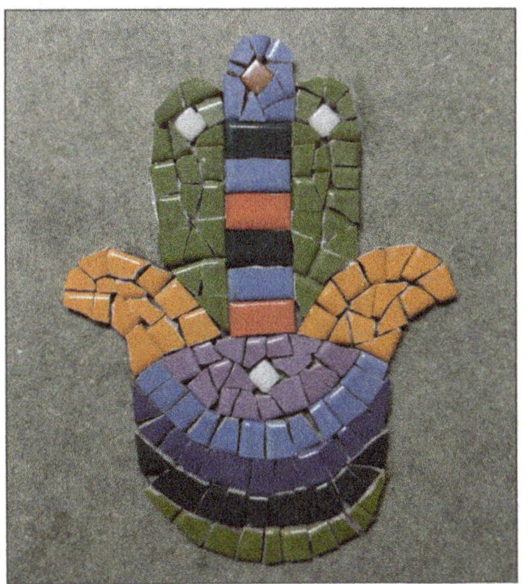

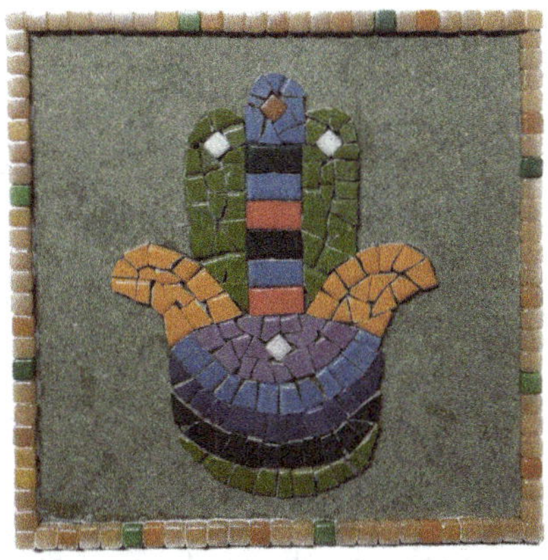

10   Cut white ceramic tiles and paste as background for the hamsa.

9   The hamsa frame will be composed of small green and orange squares. Try to keep the frame as flush as possible.

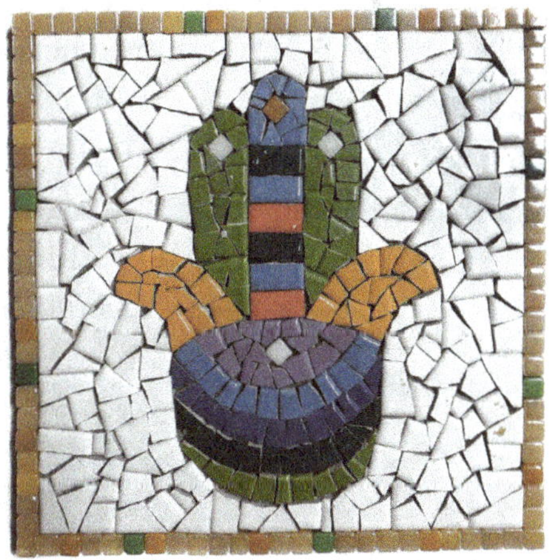

11   Wait at least a day for all glued tiles to dry properly before preparing the gray grout.

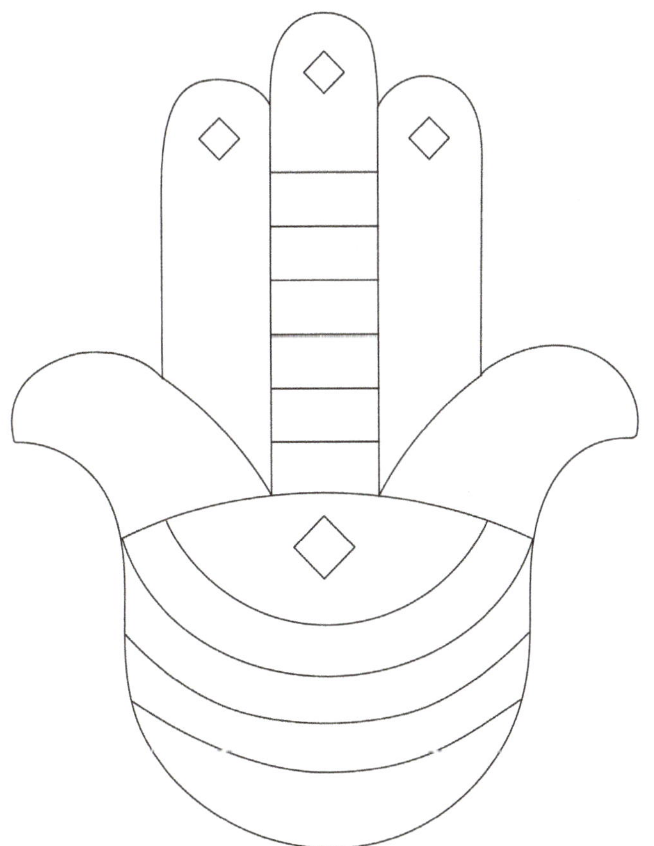

Pattern for the Hamsa:
Enlarge on a photocopier by 160% for a full size design

Applying a grout - step by step:

1 Wear a dust mask to protect your face and put on rubber gloves.

2 Cover the working surface with old newspapers.

3 Put a few spoonfuls of grout of the appropriate color (gray in this case) in a plastic bowl. If there's not enough grout, mix more grout and water in the same bowl.

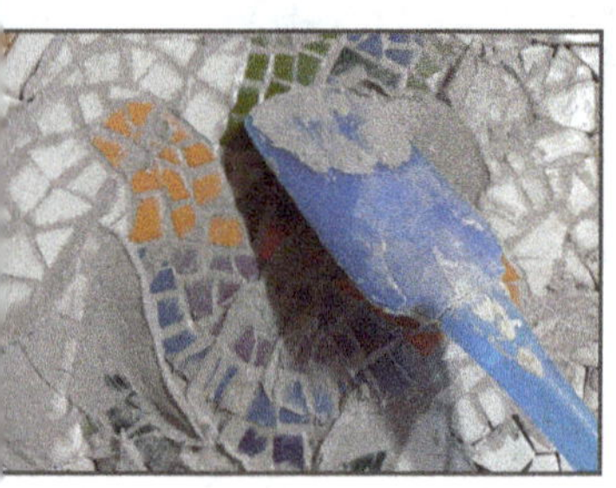

4 Pour water into the grout bowl. Mix with a wooden stick until the texture resembles a cream. Note the manufacturer's instructions.

5 Apply the grout: Pour some grout on the surface. Using a small squeegee or cake scraper, apply the grout until it fills in all slots and holes.

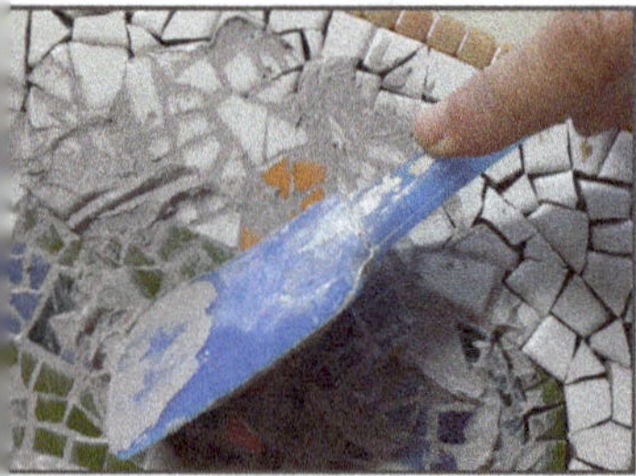

6 Once the majority of the piece is covered, use the side of the scraper to remove the excess.

7 After a few minutes when the grout starts to dry, begin cleaning: Wet the surface using a clean cotton rag or a sponge. Use a wet and dry rag several times until the work is clean. Make sure you replace the water when it becomes too mucky.

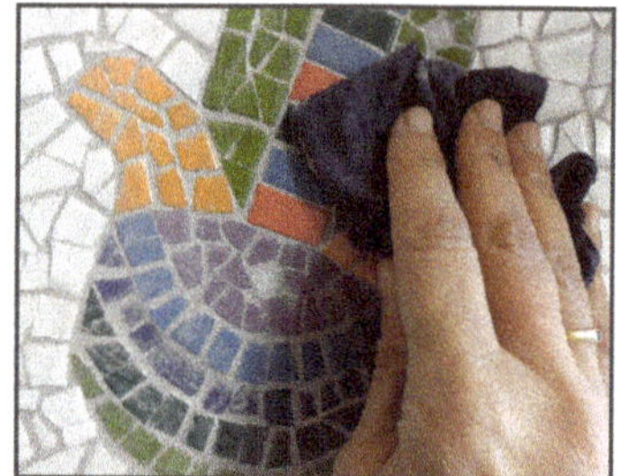

IMPORTANT: Make sure to wet the work. Wetting the grout makes the final product harder and prevents cracks. Don't skip this step!

If you've found "holes" after cleaning, fill with grout, let it dry and clean until you get a smooth and clean finish.

After the piece has dried, you can attach a hanger on the back and glue a ceramic tile on the bottom of each corner to keep it off the table surface for better insulation.

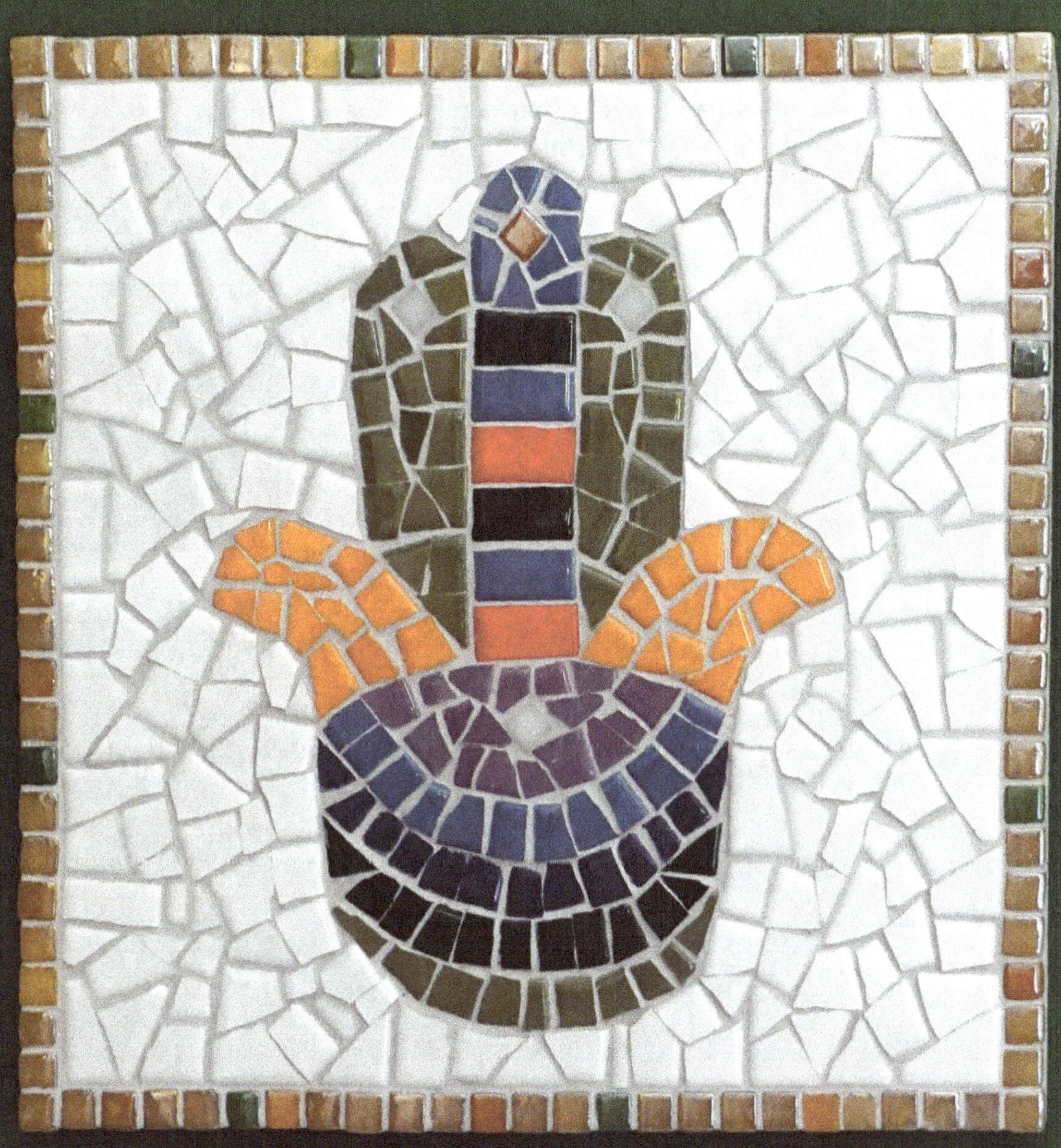

Using the Mosaic Cutter

Before cutting, wear safety goggles to protect your eyes from small fragments.

1 Hold the bottom of the cutter with your dominant hand, with the curved side facing toward the ceramic. Hold the ceramic tile in your other hand, and in your dominant hand, hold the bottom of the cutter handle.

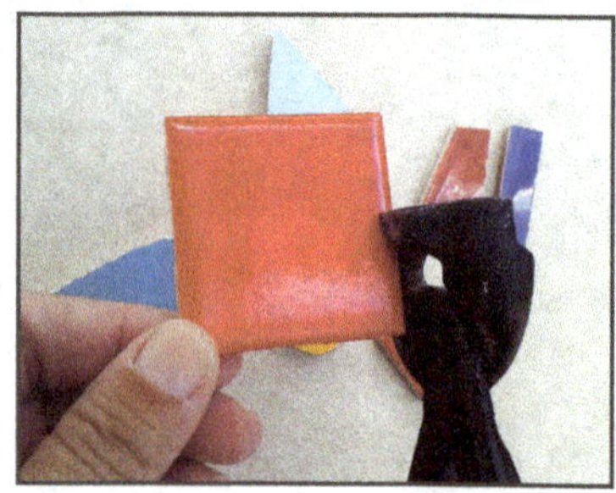

2 Hold the ceramic tile with the cutter in a straight or diagonal orientation for the type of crop you want, and clip!

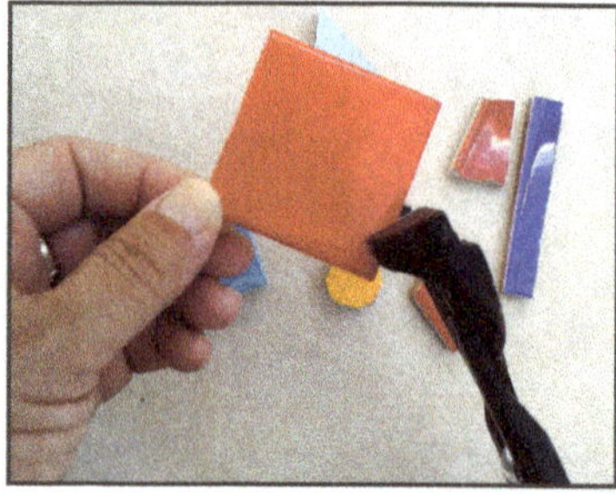

3 If you want to cut small pieces or shape the tile, hold the tile by the widest part of the cutter and clip.

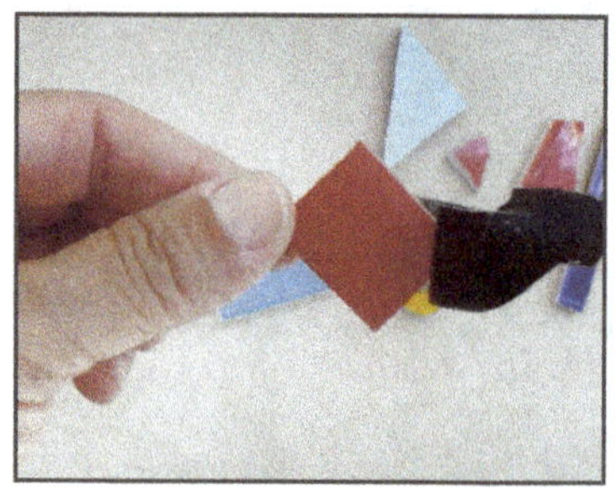

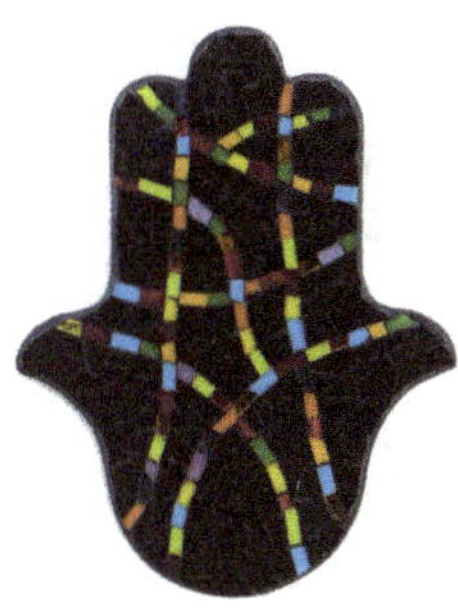

Project No. 2: Black Hamsa with a Bright Colored Stripe

Bright colors stand out on dark backgrounds. In this hamsa, we'll be using and learning how to cut shapes to a uniform width, so that they fit better into our colored stripes. You can incorporate any color you like, as long as it stands out on the black backdrop.

Working with glass panels mandates adequate cutting gear. If that isn't available, you can also work with glass squares you've cut to the right size. You can also replace the glass with ceramic, but bare in mind that glass gives off a more striking effect.

This hamsa is meant for hanging near a window, so it may shine and glow in the sunlight.

<u>Note</u>: In this book, I've exclusively used prefabricated wooden hamsas, but you can copy the hamsa contour to any square surface and add a background around it.

Materials:

A 10"/25cm high wooden hamsa (or any other size)

Several shades of colored glass – just a bit of each. You can mix matte and glossy tiles. Just remember to choose colors that will stand out from the black backdrop.

Black glass for background
PVA white glue
Paintbrush
Wheeled glass nipper
Black grout
Grout gear: Mixing bowl, water, a wooden stick, rags, gloves

1 Copy the pattern onto the hamsa surface with tracing paper.

2 Cut the colored glass to uniform-width strips (see below for detailed technique).

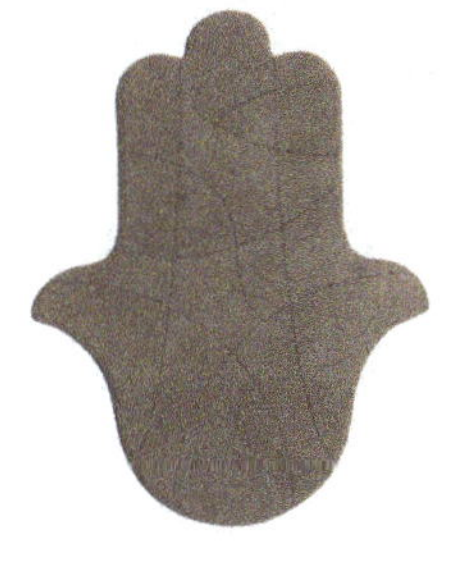

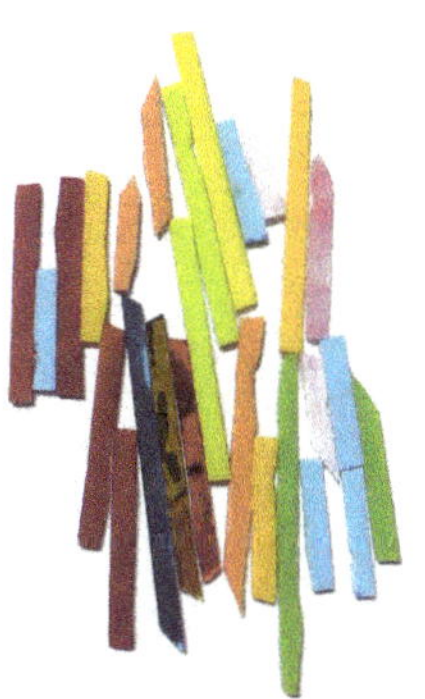

3 Cut the glass strips into small pieces measuring about 0.4-0.6"/1-1.5cm.

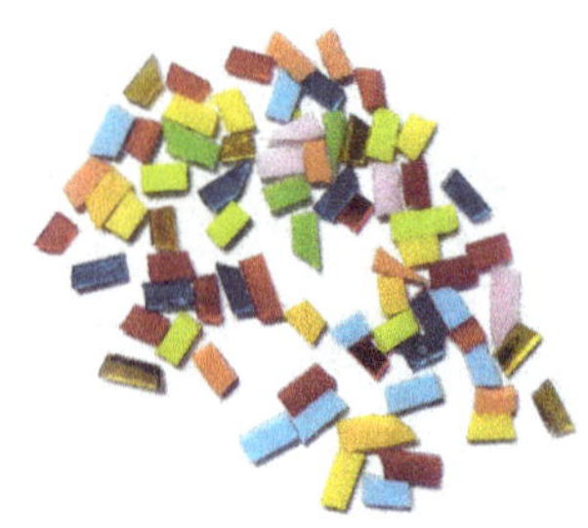

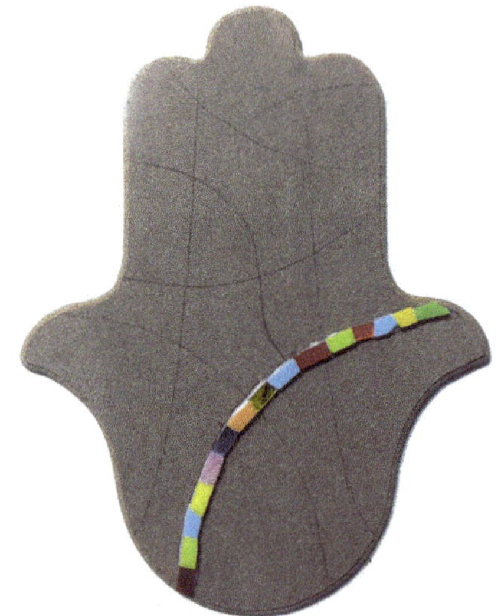

4 Using a brush and glue, paste colored pieces along the strips, with a different color for each piece. When gluing rectangles on an arch, you'll sometimes need to snip an edge to make it connect better to the adjacent piece.

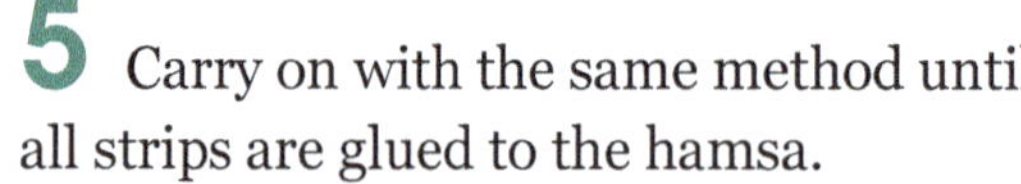

5 Carry on with the same method until all strips are glued to the hamsa.

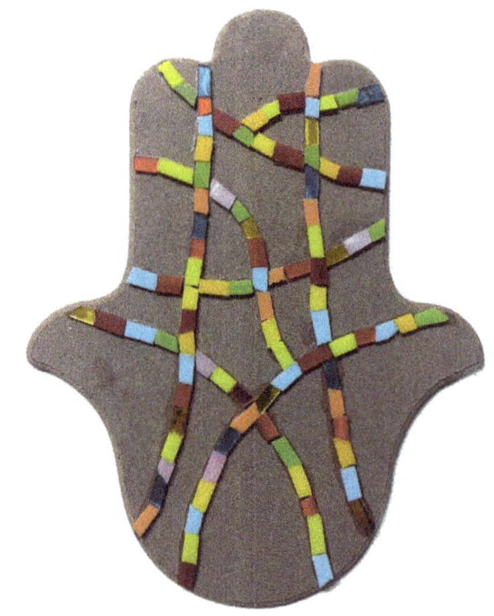

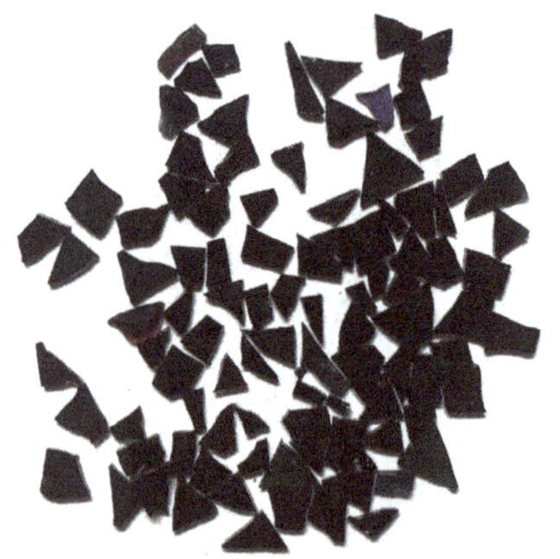

6 Cut black glass into small random pieces.

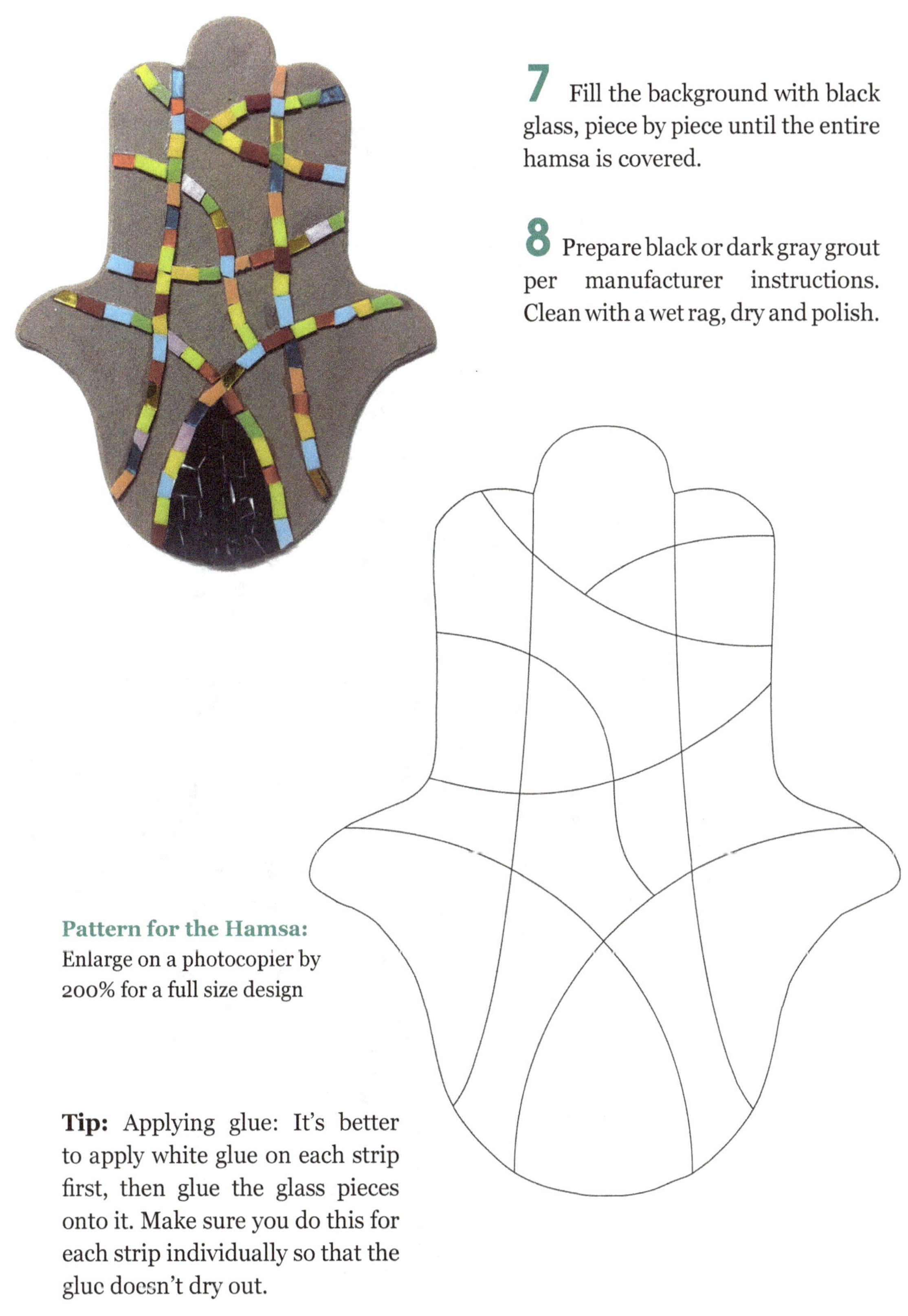

7 Fill the background with black glass, piece by piece until the entire hamsa is covered.

8 Prepare black or dark gray grout per manufacturer instructions. Clean with a wet rag, dry and polish.

Pattern for the Hamsa:
Enlarge on a photocopier by 200% for a full size design

Tip: Applying glue: It's better to apply white glue on each strip first, then glue the glass pieces onto it. Make sure you do this for each strip individually so that the gluc doesn't dry out.

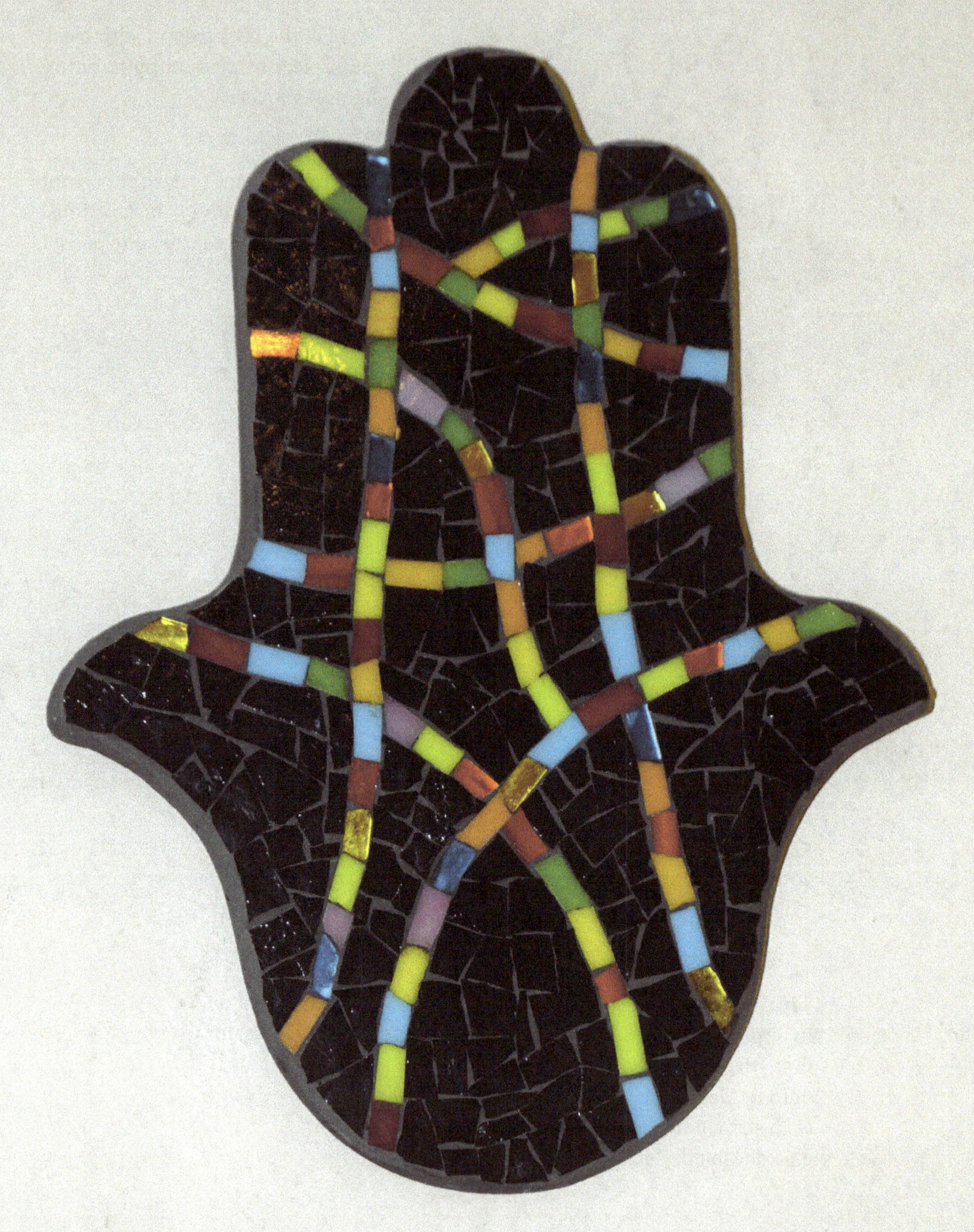

This pattern can be created with various colors and combinations.

See for instance the hamsa below, white with blue strips. For the backdrop, I've used white glass tiles with a seashell effect which I cut into different shape pieces. The strips were composed of glass pieces, blue beads and polymer clay flowers.

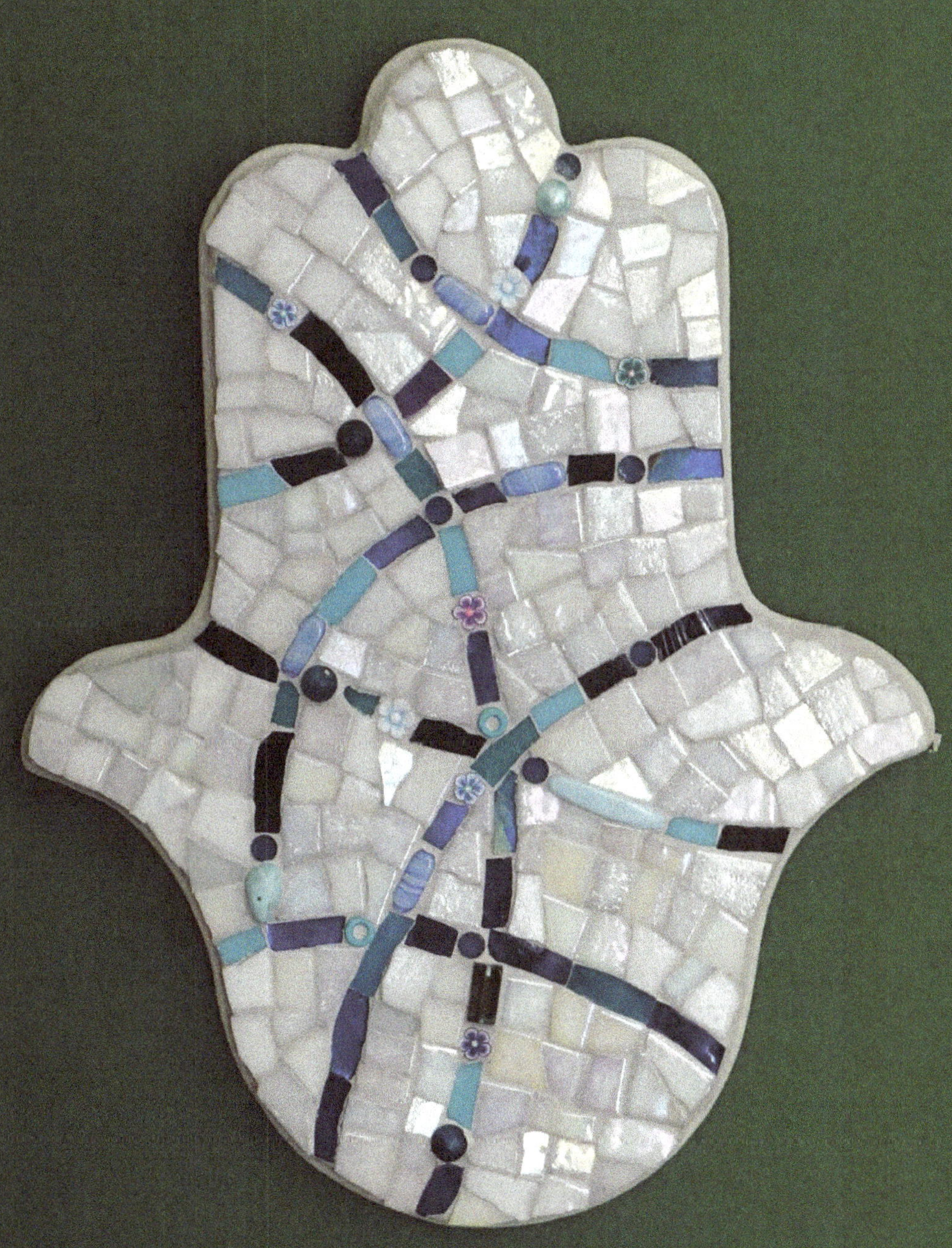

Cutting Glass into Strips

The technique for cutting glass is different than with ceramics. Here, we score the glass with a blade, then separate the two pieces.

Stained glass and mosaic artist use these glass cutting techniques, and to achieve maximum accuracy, each piece is machine-sanded after cutting. In this book, we'll only be using the blade and nipper.

There are several types of blades and hand grips. It's recommended that you use a quality cutter to make prolonged work more comfortable.

In order to cut accurate glass strips, use the cutting blade, L-square and pliers.

First, we will learn how to use the cutter.

1. Place the panel you want to cut on a clean, level surface.

2. In order to cut a straight, accurate line, use a framing square or T-square: Place the square on the line you wish to cut.

3. Hold the glass cutter with your dominant hand and dip it in oil if necessary (required with certain types of cutters).

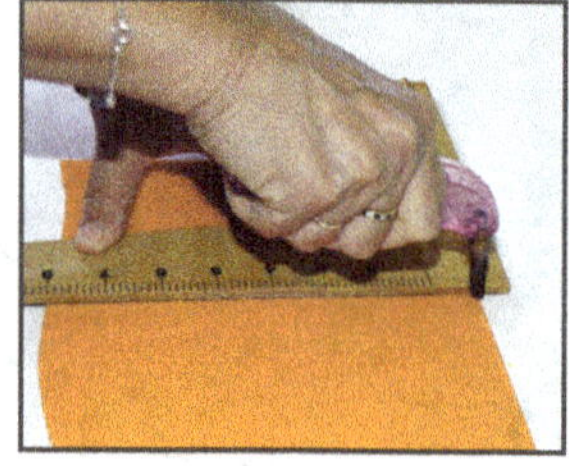

4. Place the cutter at the top or bottom edge of the glass and hold it straight, perpendicular to the glass.

5. Score the glass lengthwise with your dominant hand, while pressing on the square with your other hand to keep it in place. You can cut either from top to bottom or vice-versa. It's essential to do this while maintaining even pressure from edge to edge, otherwise the cut might become crooked. If you hear a slight ripping sound, you're doing it right.

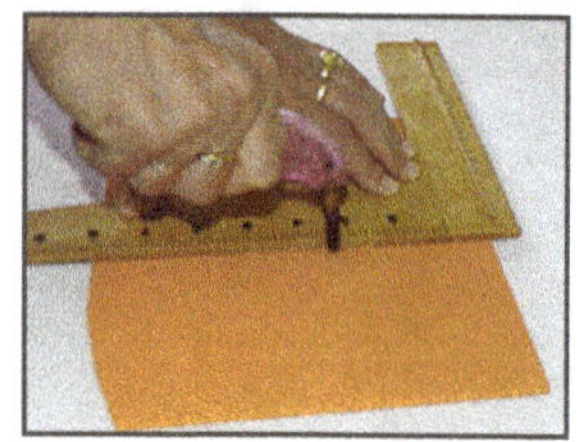

6. Grab the glass by its bottom with running plier and snap it off. Note that the markings in the pliers are facing upward. The glass will snap in two along the line.

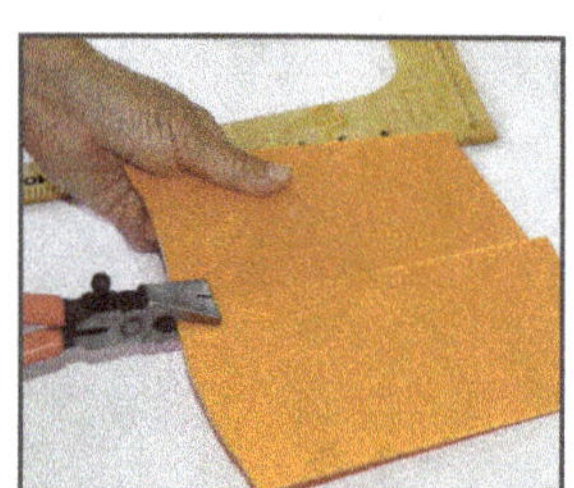

Cutting Glass into Strips by Size:

1. Place the glass you wish to cut on a clean, level surface.

2. Using a glass marker and T-square, mark the width you want to cut. You can mark all the desired lines in advance.

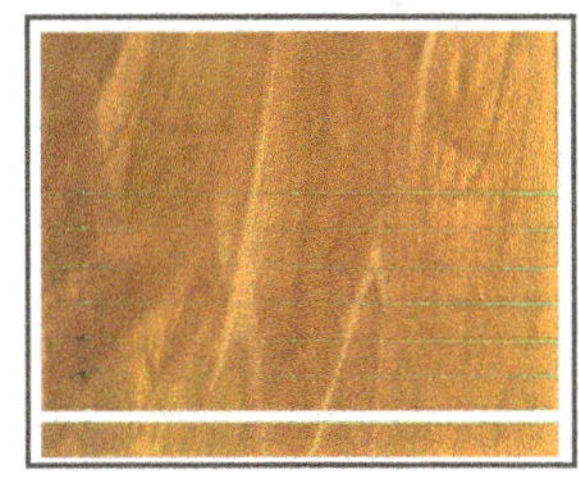

3. Place the T-square on the glass. Begin cutting the strips in order as explained before. Leave the wide part of the glass for last. Repeat stages 3-6 of glass cutting

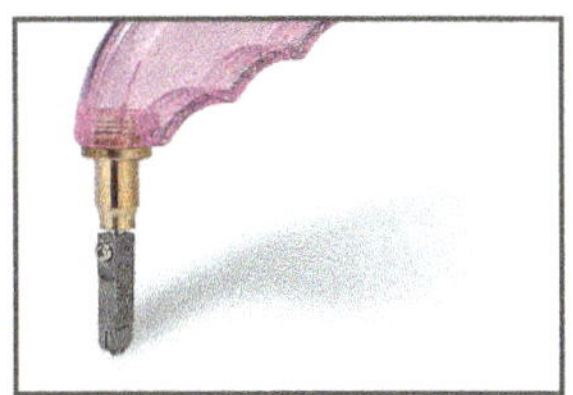

Cutting Glass into Strips with a Square Object:

Another method of cutting straight strips is using a small square with the proper width. This will save you measuring and marking hassle. Note that the strip cut will be narrower than the square, due to the blade's thickness.

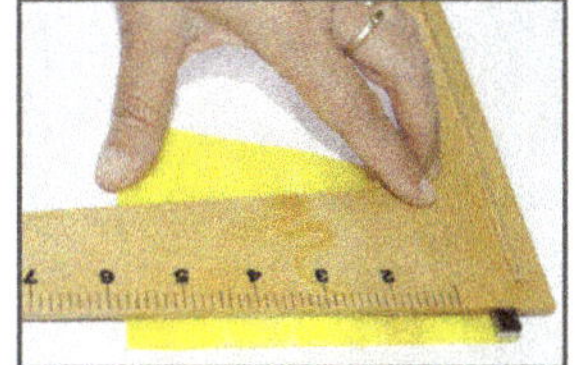

1. Align the square with the top side of the glass. Place the square object adjacent to the square, so that it's flush with the edge of the glass.

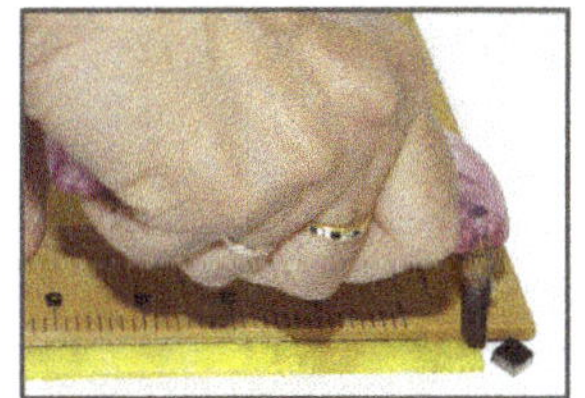

2. Remove the square object, groove the glass with the cutter and snap the strip.

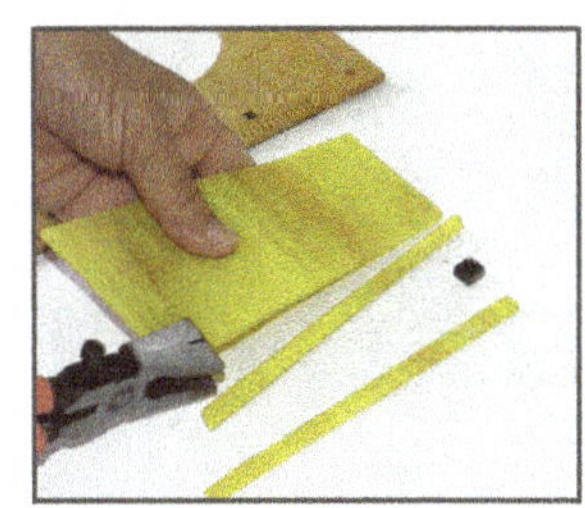

3. Repeat this action for every individual cut. If you maintain accuracy, the strips will be uniform in size and you won't need to mark out lines at all.

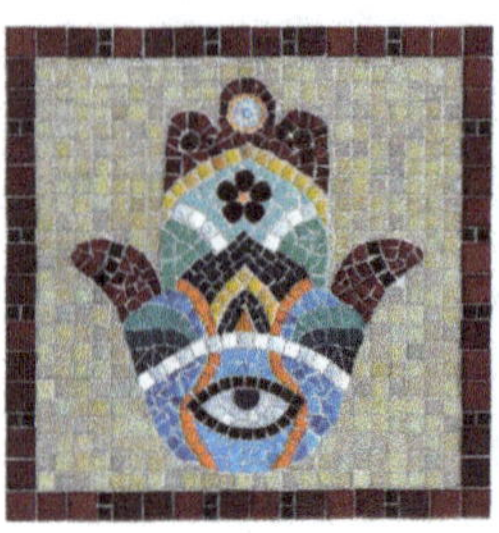

Project No. 3: Hamsa Picture Frame

This hamsa combines the traditional eye motif and the color blue, meant to ward off the evil eye and protect the home. It may look like a complex and arduous task, but we'll take it step-by-step with detailed explanations for each step.

I've already told you that I like incorporating various materials into mosaic work. E.g. two coins painted black to decorate the top of the fingers, a flower made from ceramic "droplets", or prefabricated round pieces. Everything else is cut or whole glass and ceramic squares in various sizes, which create a special harmonic composition.

I've added a decorated frame from ceramic tiles so there's no need for a frame – just make a sturdy hanger and find a good location on the wall.

Materials:

A wooden board measuring 40x40 cm/15.7"x15.7"

Glass and ceramic tiles in shades of red, orange, green, turquoise, azure and white

Off-white glass tiles measuring 1.5x1.5 cm/0.6"x0.6"

Black, white and gray tiles measuring 1x1 cm/0.39"x0.39"

Red tiles measuring 2.5x2.5 cm/0.98"x0.98"

Black tiles measuring 1x1 cm/0.39"x0.39"

Coins/beads/etc.

PVA white glue

Paintbrush

Wheeled glass nipper

Tile cutter

Gray Grout

Grout Gear: Mixing bowl, water, a wooden stick, rags, gloves

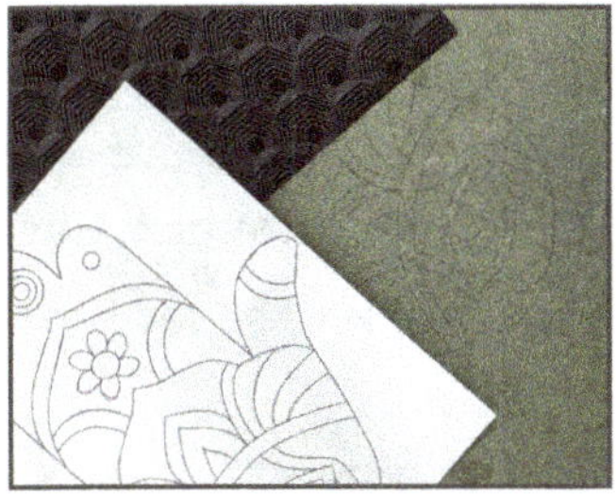

1 Copy the hamsa pattern onto the wooden board with tracing paper.

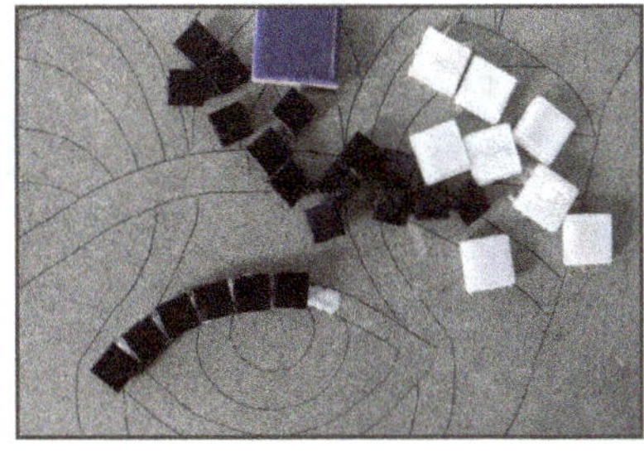

2 Begin the hamsa from the eye: First create the frame from small black squares. Make sure you align the squares by their bottom side to form a nice-looking arch.

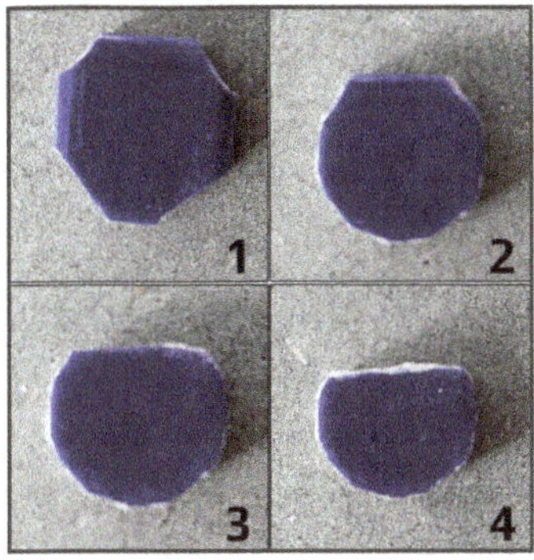

3 For the pupil, use a blue square and snip it into a circle: First snip the four corners (1), then use the nipper to round off the cuts (2) except for the top, which you should leave straight (3). Then, use the nipper to make the top flush to get the desired pupil size.

4 The inside of the eye should be crafted from white rectangles, cutting some of the slightly diagonally as seen in the picture to reduce spaces in the arch. First, glue the line closest to the pupil. Then glue the rest to prevent any movement.

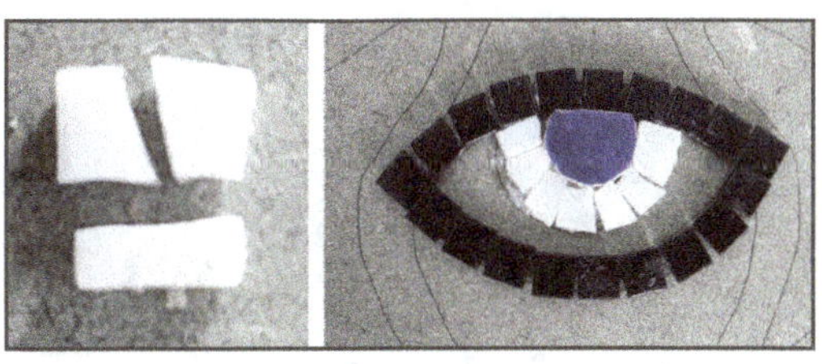

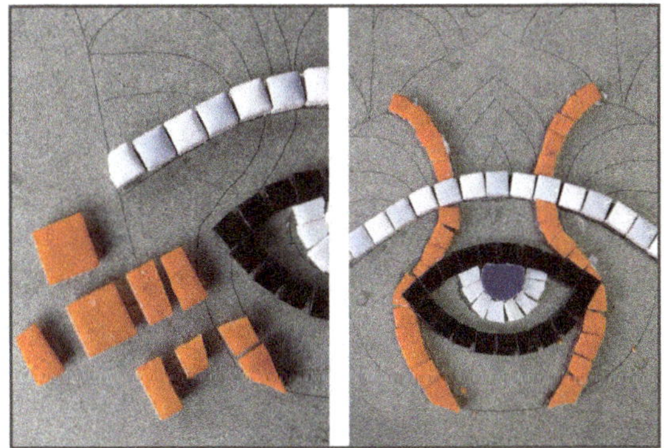

5 Craft the two orange strips from squares cut into strips. Here as well, you should incorporate diagonal pieces to create a nice rounded line. Create an arch above the eye using white and gray square.

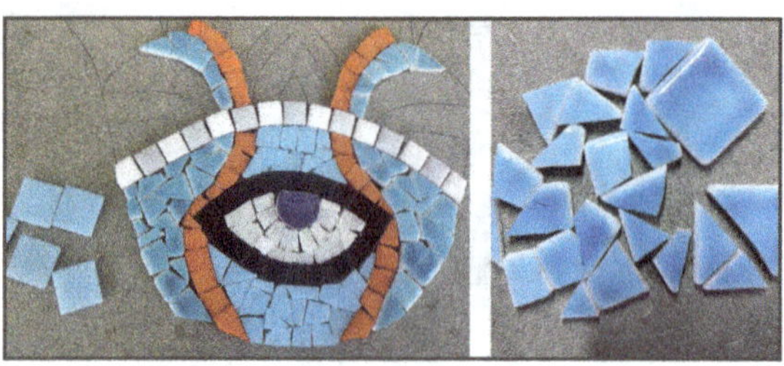

6 Complete another row of white tiles in the eye and fill out the area with turquoise tiles cut into random pieces.

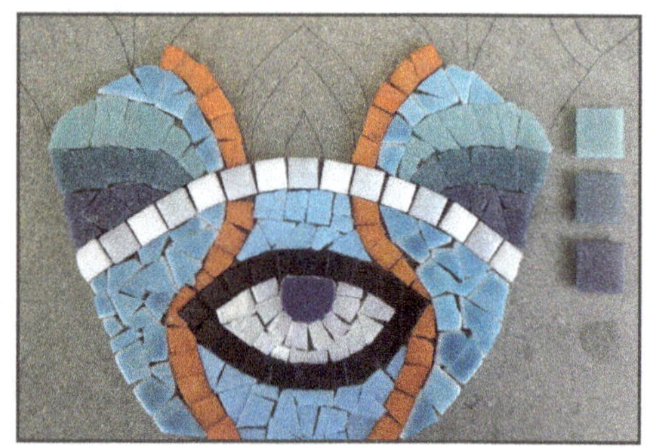

7 Fill the area above the eye in three shades of green/turquoise.

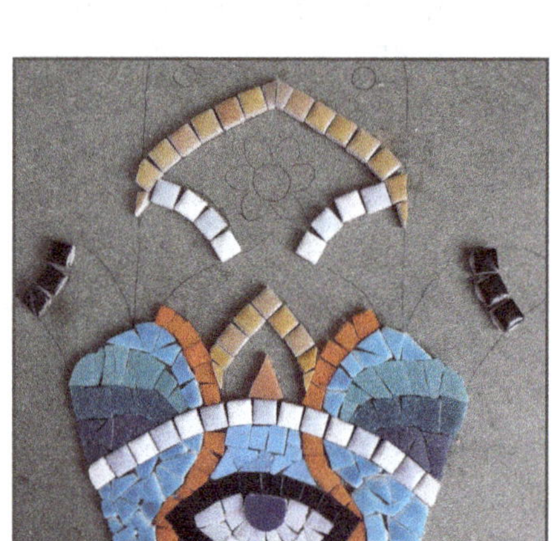

8 Glue an orange triangle. Create the arches seen in the photo from small white and bright orange squares, and use black for the middle of the lateral fingers. Here as well, it's recommended that you wait until these pieces are fully dried, and only then move on to pasting around them.

9 On the two lateral fingers, glue cut red/maroon shards.

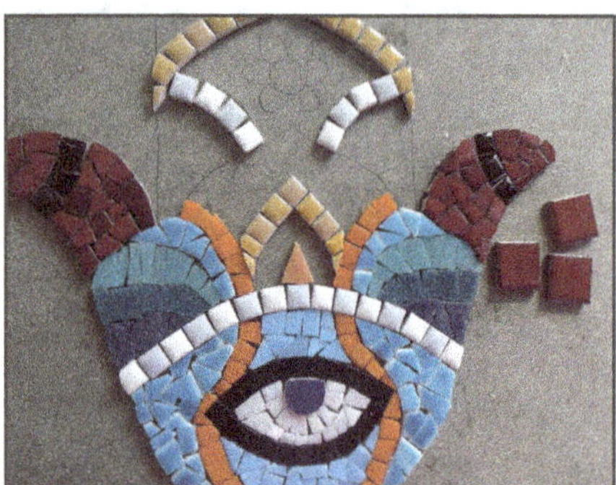

10 Inside the arches, glue cut turquoise + dark green tiles for the strips, and for the sides use green + light turquoise.

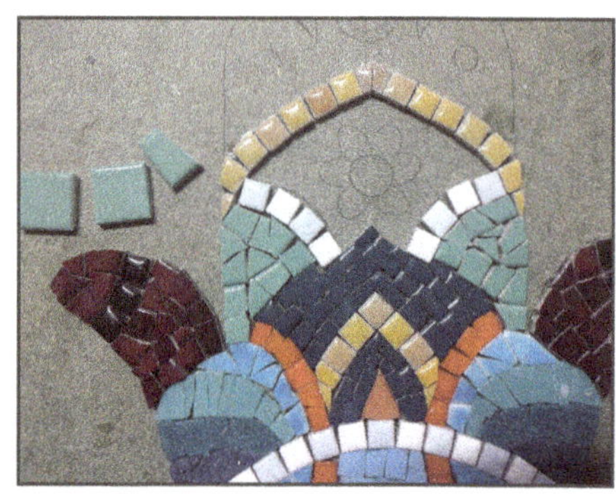

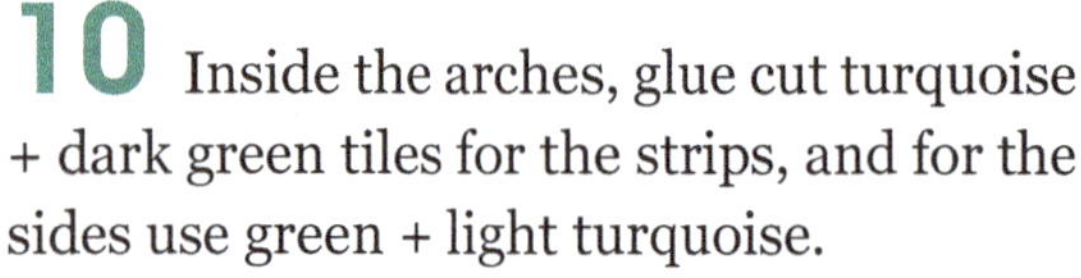

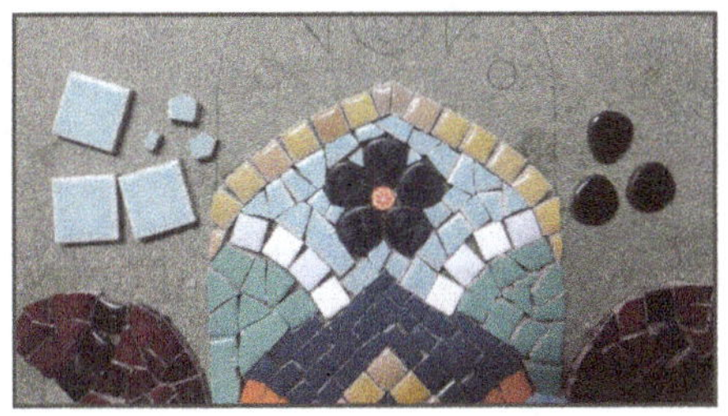

11 Inside the upper arch, paste a flower. At the center of my flower, I paste an orange polymer clay circle, and used droplet-shaped blue tile for the leaves. The background is azure cut tiles.

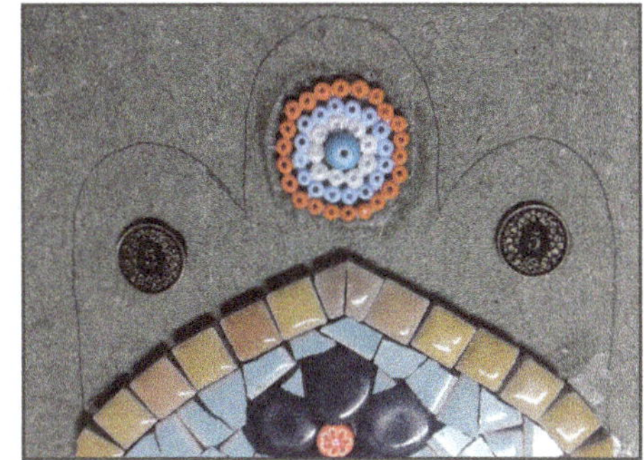

12 To make things more interesting, I glued two coins at the top of the hamsa, and in the center I crafted a circle from rows of tiny orange, white and azure beads.

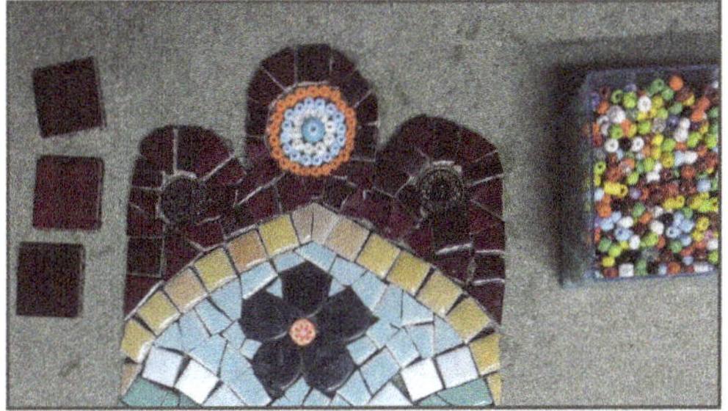

13 To complete the fingers, glue small bits of red tile.

14 The frame is composed of red tiles with small black squares between them. Make sure you paste the frame so it's flush and close to the edges.

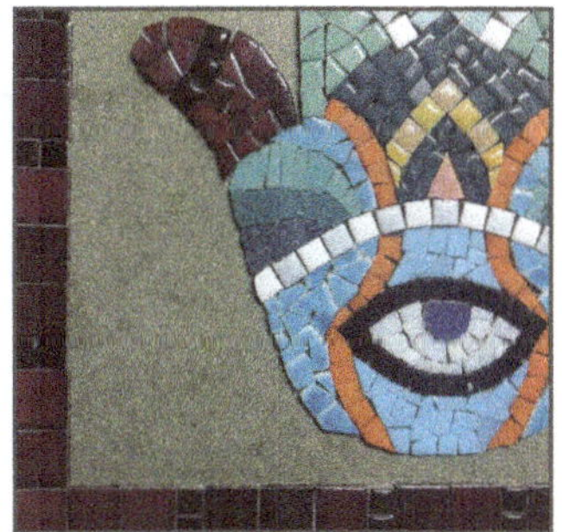

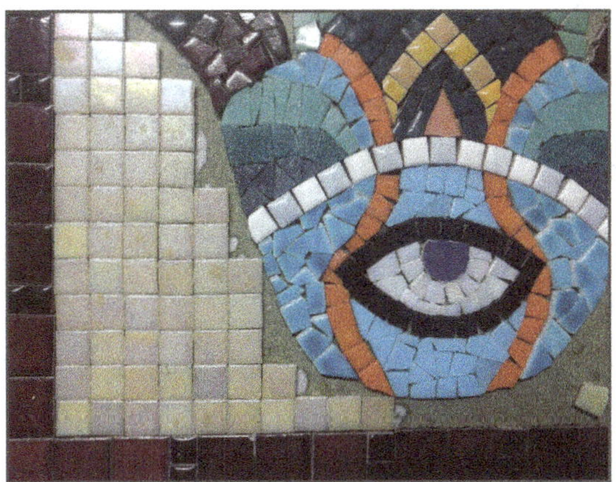

15 After the frame is fully dried, fill it with cream-colored squares. Glass squares will give a glossier and more brilliant look. Paste the whole squares first, then cut them into triangles and fill out the vacant spots. Make sure you keep the rows straight.

16 Prepare cream/off-white grout according to manufacturer instructions and apply across the picture. Use a scraper to apply the grout all the way to the edges as well. Clean thoroughly with a wet rag.

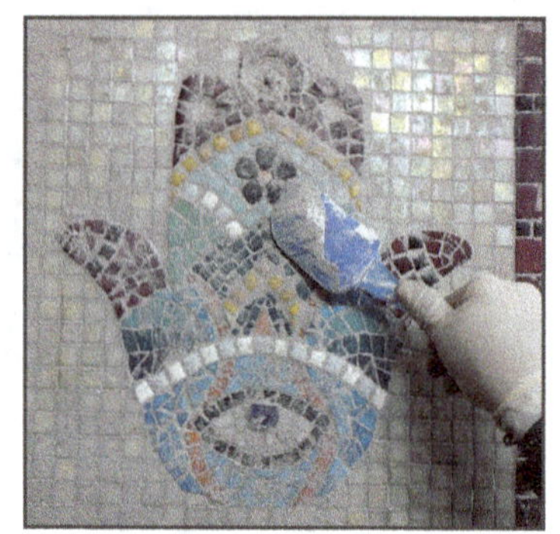

17 The picture is ready! No need to frame, just add a sturdy hanger at the back and find a nice spot to hang it in.

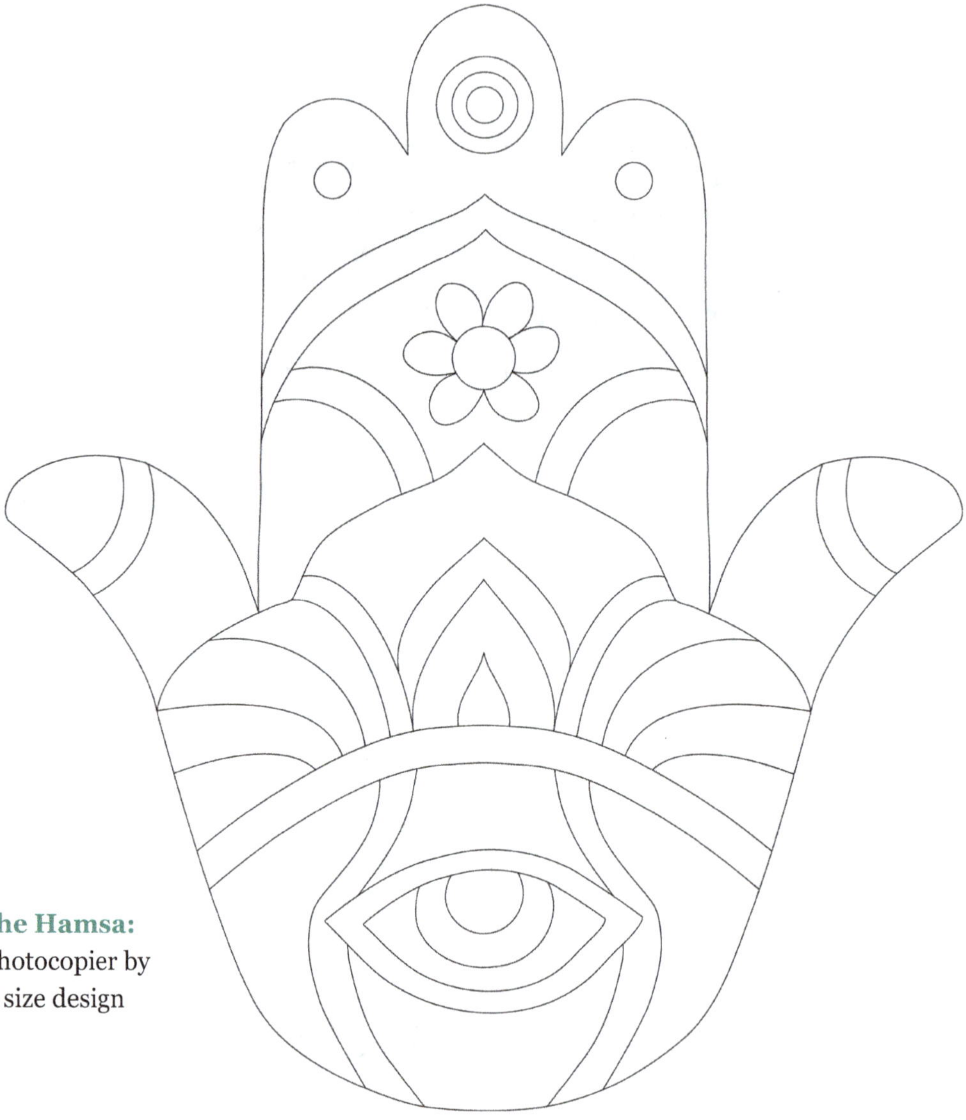

Pattern for the Hamsa:
Enlarge on a photocopier by
210% for a full size design

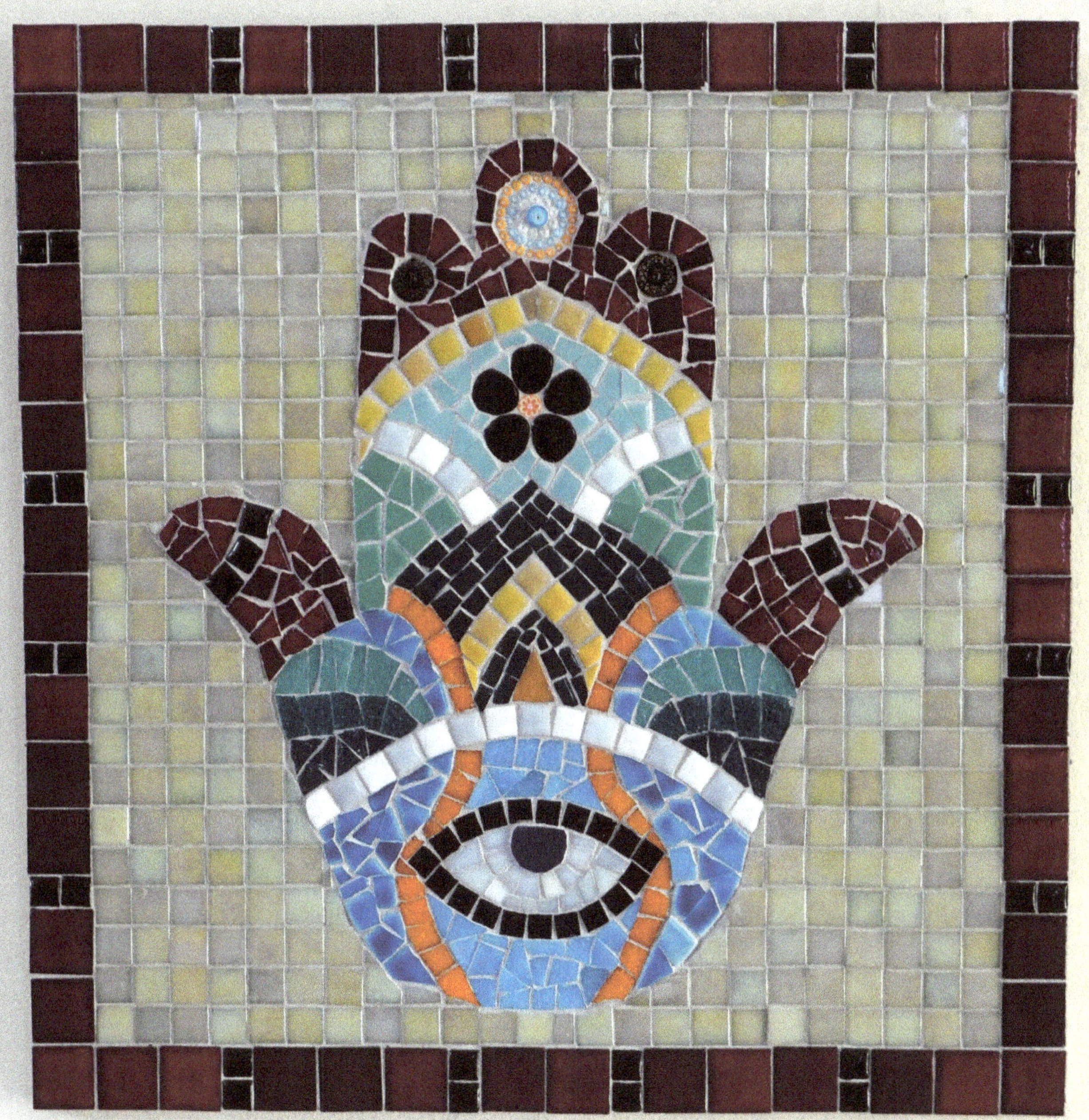

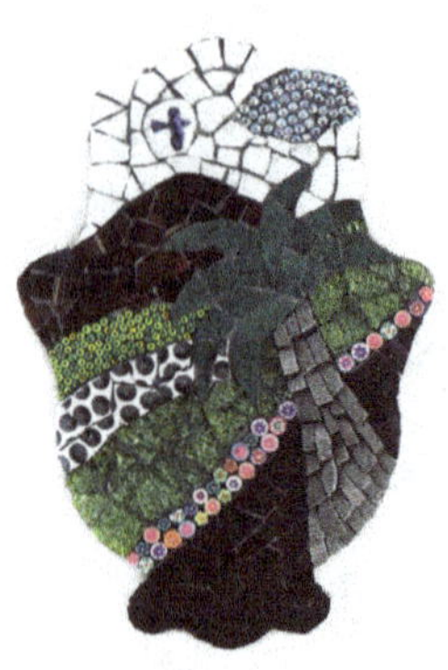

Project No. 4: Grout-less Hamsa with Various Media

Most mosaic works have two stages: The gluing and grout preparation. I enjoy incorporating various materials into the mosaic, and sometimes worry that they'll lose their luster during the grout stage, or that I won't be able to clean them properly. For instance, when using jewelry, special beads or elements with rough textures.

The hamsa below with the pine scene was created from various materials with colored tile glue. It's important that the glue is thick enough so that it would fill the cracks between the mosaic pieces.

Materials:

Wooden hamsa measuring 11.4"/29cm in height (or any other size)
Green, brown, white and gray crockery
Brown glass
Small green and yellow beads
Polymer clay flowers

Cylinder-shaped glossy beads
Tweezers
Wheeled glass nipper
Wooden stick
Tile adhesive
Screwdriver
Wet rag or wet wipes

1 Copy the hamsa pattern to the wooden board using tracing paper.

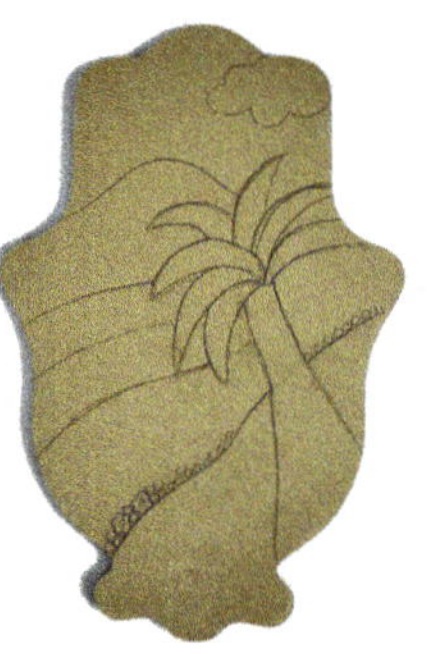

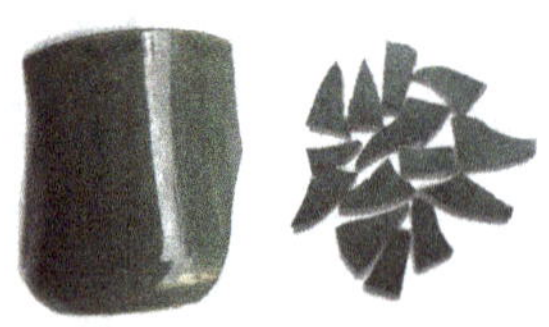

2 Using the nipper, cut a green glass into triangular and trapezoidal pieces for the palm leaves. See below for instructions on using the nipper to cut crockery.

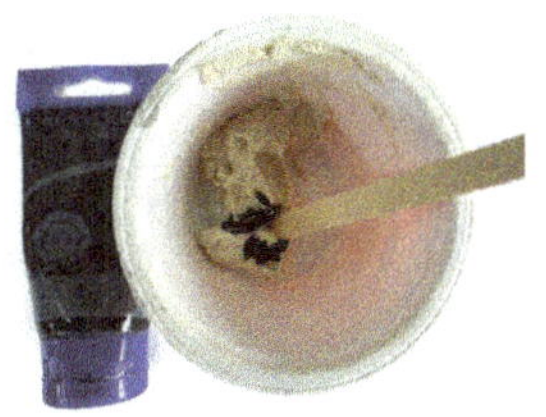

3 Before pasting, prepare the glue: Mix some tile glue with black acrylic paint in a small bowl until a uniform dark gray mixture is formed. It's better to prepare several small batches instead of one large one, as the glue tends to dry quickly.

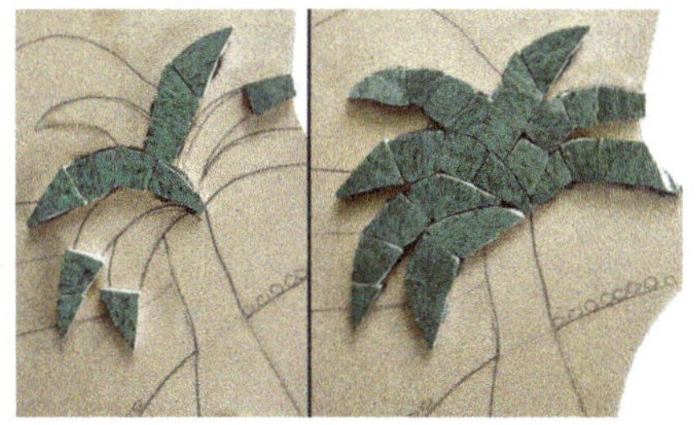

4 Begin with the palm leaves: Paste the triangular pieces at the edge of each leaf. Then fill in the leaves piece by piece to get the right shape. It's advised that you apply the glue on each piece individually to keep the work tidy.

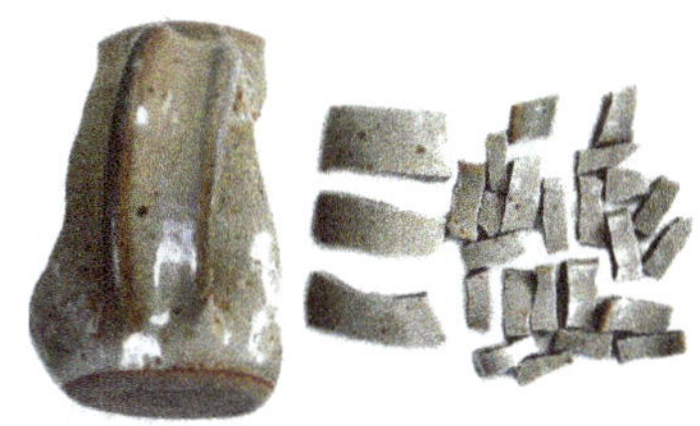

5 Cut gray glass (ceramic can also be used) into rectangular pieces to a more or less uniform width. Cut the glass lengthwise with the nipper, then cut into wide strips, and finally cut those into little pieces.

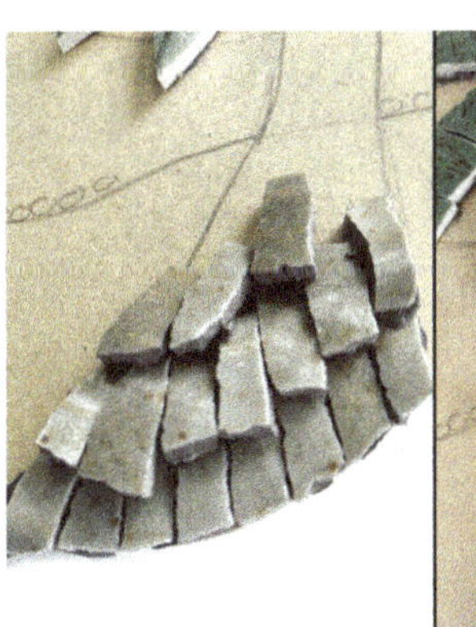
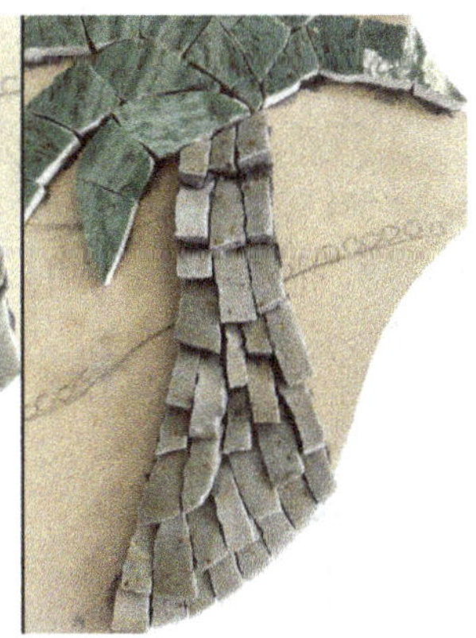

6 The palm trunk will be crafted from "shingles" – slightly overlapping rectangular pieces. Make sure to remove residual glue.

7 Cut a brown dish into small random pieces.

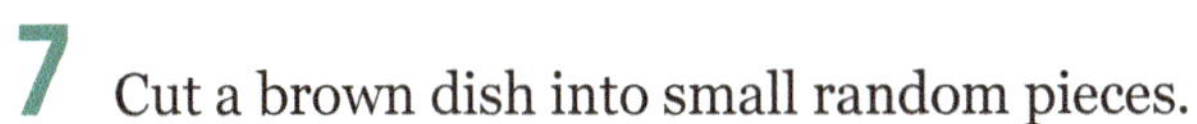
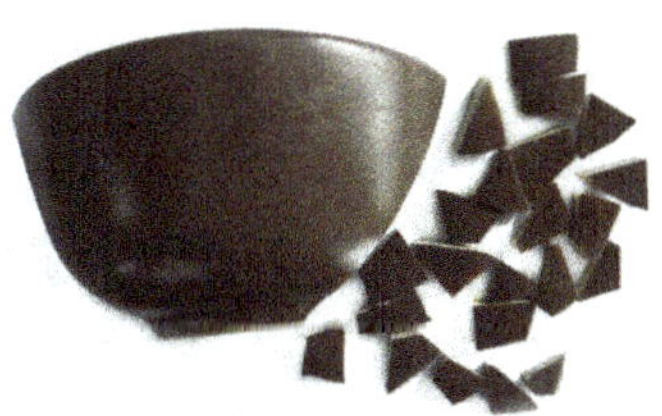

8 Paste the brown pieces on the bottom part of the hamsa. Here you can apply glue directly to the surface and then place the pieces as close together as possible. Add lines using polymer clay circles.

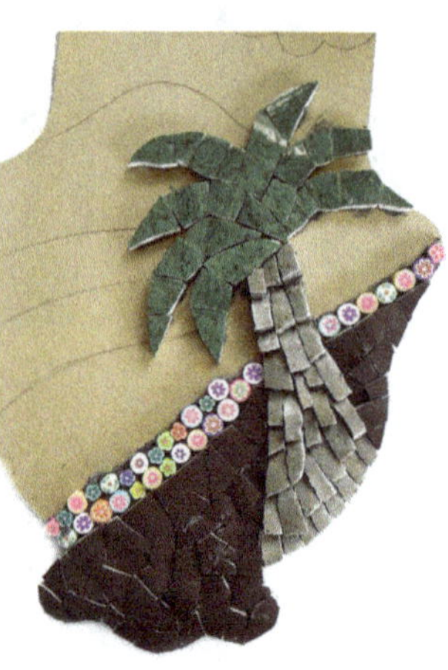

9 For the green part of the hamsa, I used glass tiles that were rough on one side and smooth on the other. Cut the green glass you picked into small random pieces.

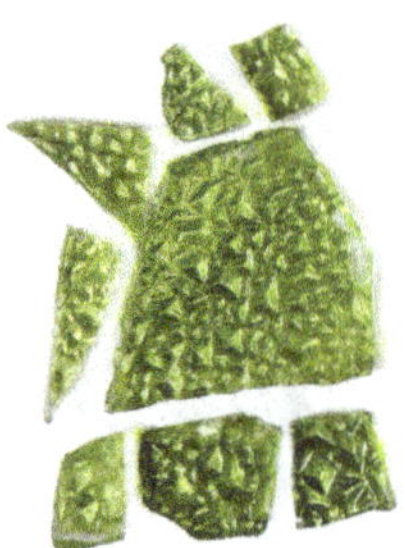

10 For this piece, I chose to glue the green glass with the smooth side on top.

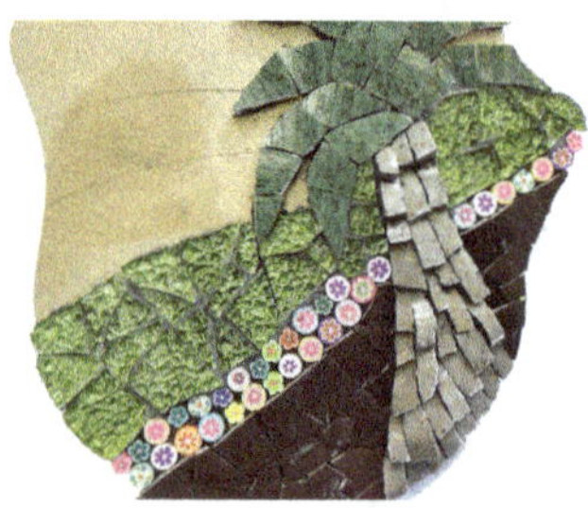

11 For the next area, I used a small polka-dot bowl, which I gradually cut into small pieces.

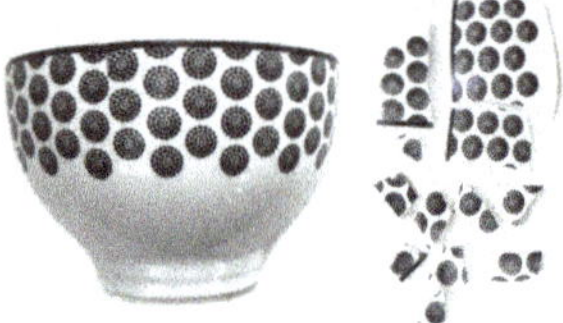

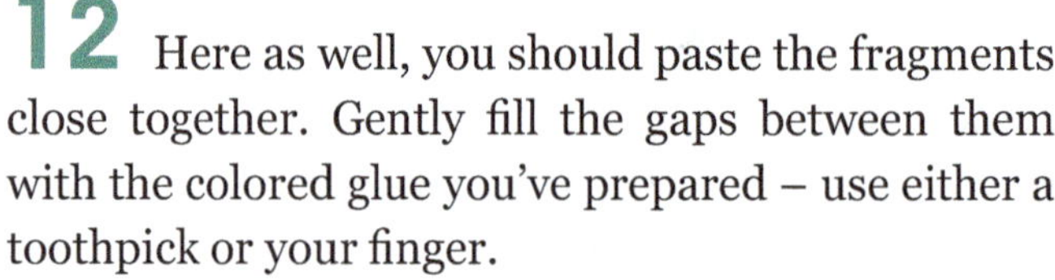

12 Here as well, you should paste the fragments close together. Gently fill the gaps between them with the colored glue you've prepared – use either a toothpick or your finger.

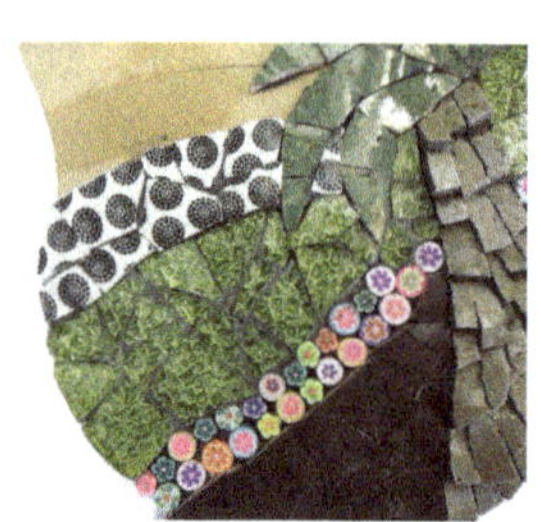

13 Now for the tiny beads: Fill a small bowl with green and yellow beads. Apply glue to a small surface and use tweezers to arrange the beads tightly onto the glue.

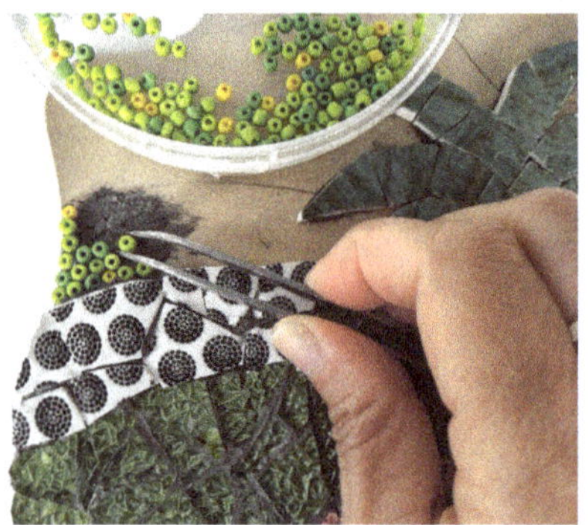

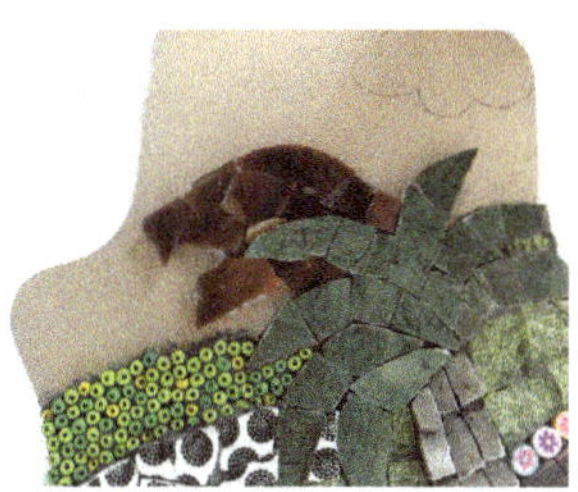

14 Cut brown glass into small pieces and paste over the mountain area.

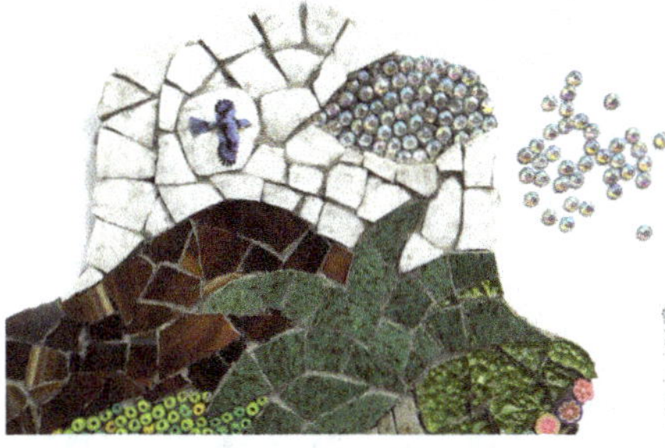

15 The cloud is composed of flat, round, shiny beads pasted close together. Use a bright color for the backdrop. I used a glass with bright inscriptions and added a bird symbol that was engraved on it.

16 The hamsa is done! Time to clean up and add some glue to smooth out surfaces where necessary.

Tip: Keep the work clean at all times – scrape off leftover glue with a wet rag or small screwdriver. It gets much harder to clean when it dries up.

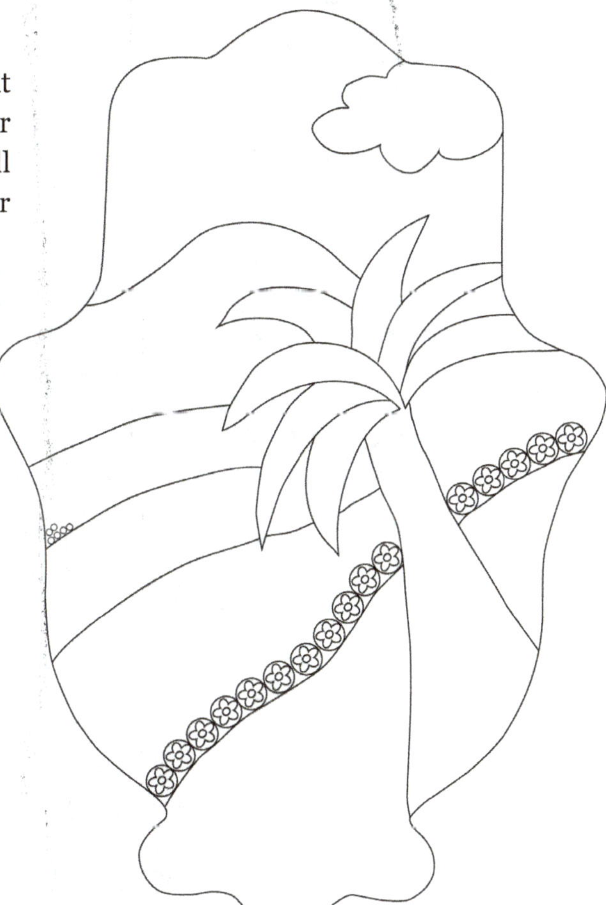

Pattern for the Hamsa:
Enlarge on a photocopier by 240% for a full size design

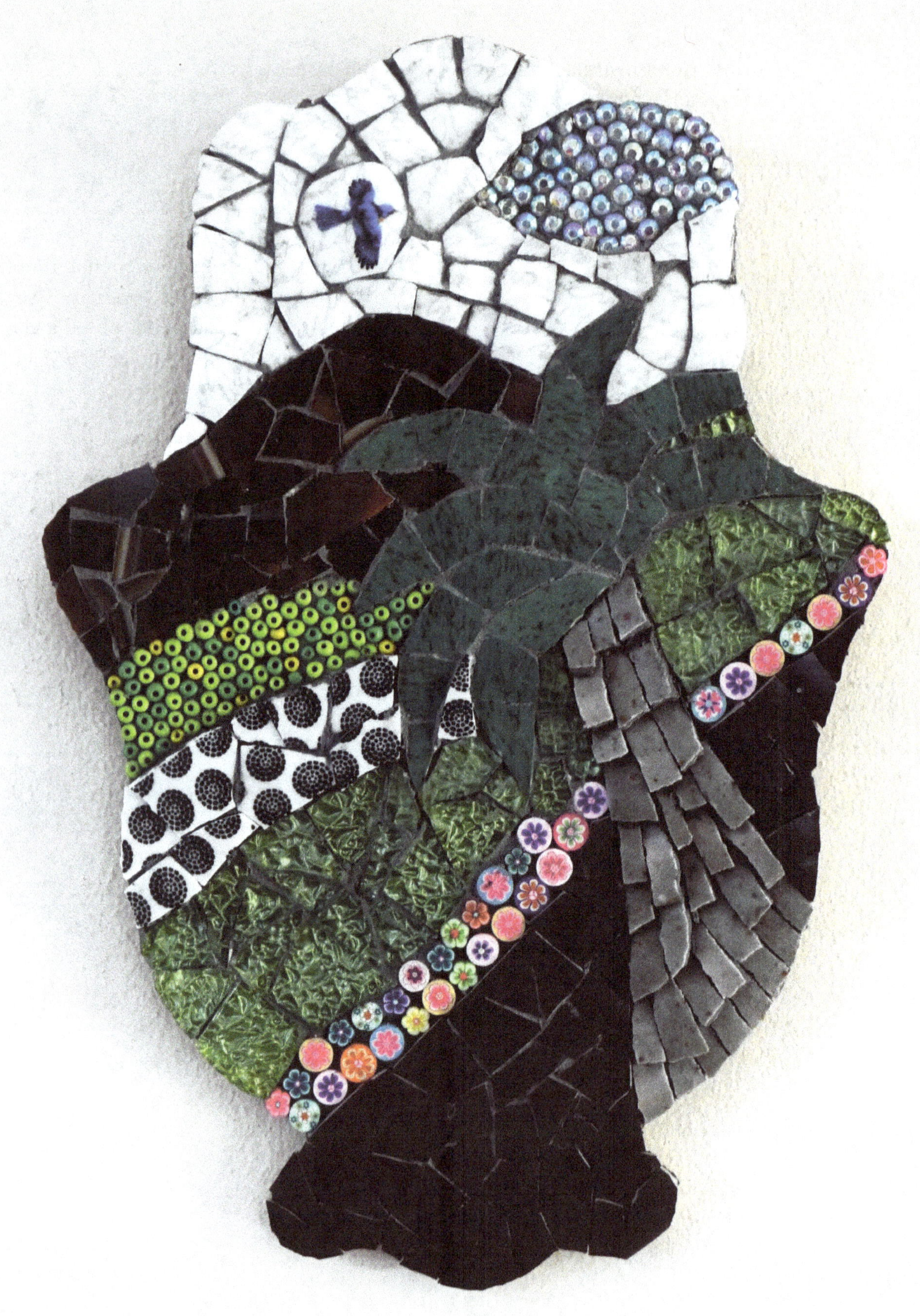

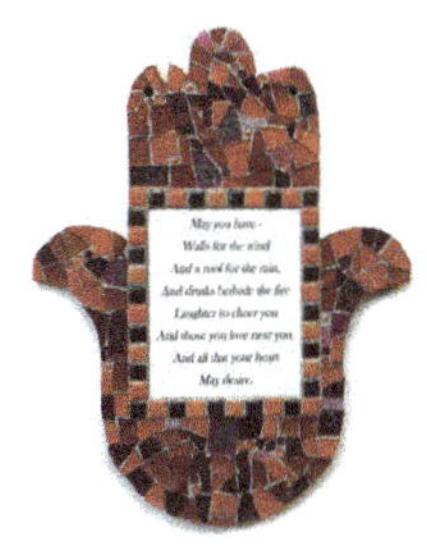

Project No. 5: Hamsa with Home Blessing

I like incorporating original texts into mosaic, and have often used printed ceramic tiles for that purpose. However, printing on tiles is expensive and not readily available to everyone. Thus, I've searched and found an easy method for you to incorporate in mosaic (not just hamsas) any inscription you wish – poems, blessings, etc. All you need is a printer, sticker paper, a piece of glass and clear wallpaper. Sounds like a hassle? Not really – see below for step-by-step instructions.

Now you can craft a hamsa with a housewarming poem, a funny limerick or any other idea you come up with.

Materials:

A wooden Hamsa measuring 30cm/12"
Black and Red tiles measuring 1 x 1 cm/0.39"x0.39"
Red glass shards in several shades
Clear glass
Text printed on white sticker paper
Clear wallpaper

PVA white glue
Paintbrush
Wheeled glass nipper
Glass cutter
T-ruler
Dark gray grout
Grout Gear: Mixing bowl, water, a wooden stick, rags, gloves

1 Print the appropriate size text on sticker paper. Use a blade to cut a rectangle or square (try printing the text with a frame to align your cut with).

2 Carefully glue the sticker onto clear glass. Try to align it to the one corner to make the subsequent cut easier.

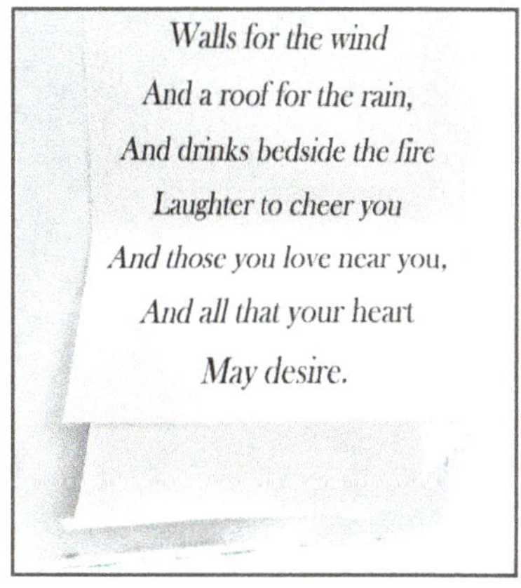

3   Using a glass cutter and a ruler, cut the glass around the sticker.

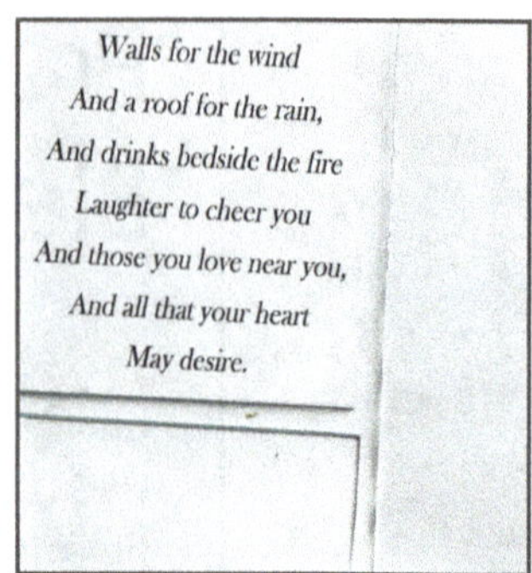

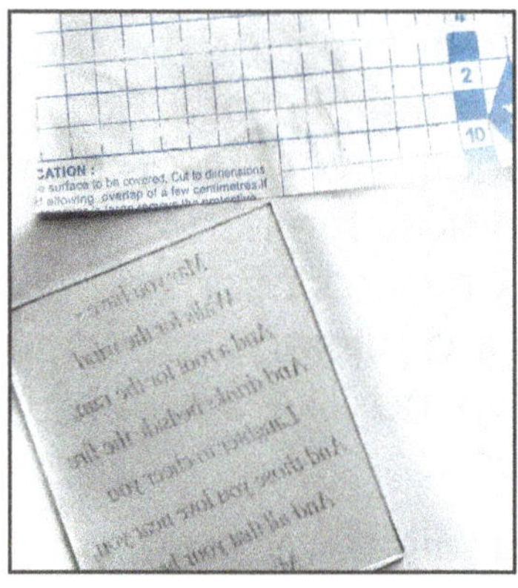

4   Cut a piece of clear wallpaper roughly 2 cm larger than the glass panel. Peel off the wallpaper and lay on the table sticky side up. At the center, place the text facing down.

5   Fold over the wallpaper edges like an envelope and tighten well (a diagonal cut is easier to fold).

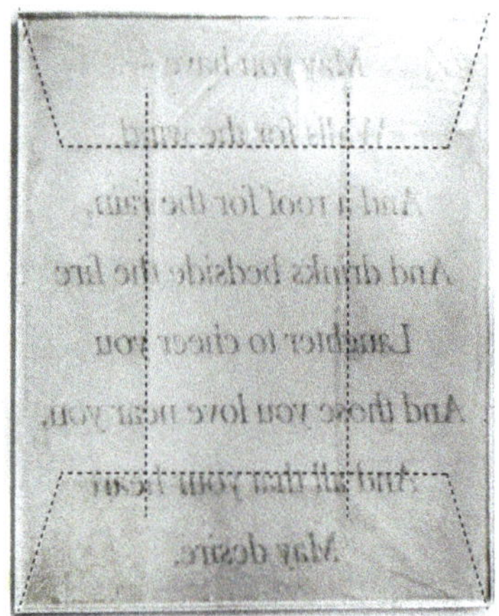

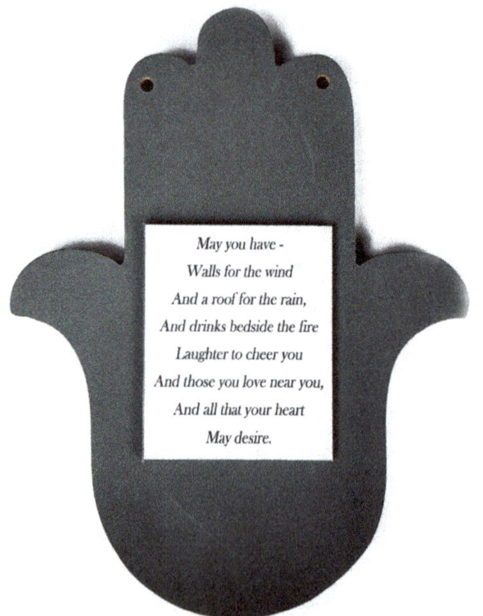

6   Paste the text at the center of the hamsa.

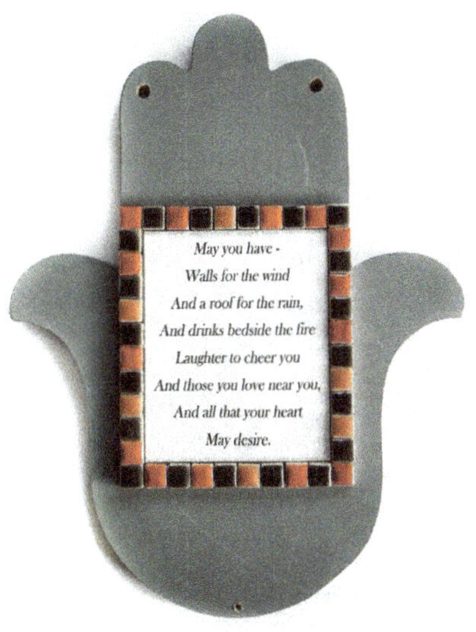

7 Paste a frame from red and black squares around the text.

8 Prepare shards of red glass in different shades. You can add beads to the mix.

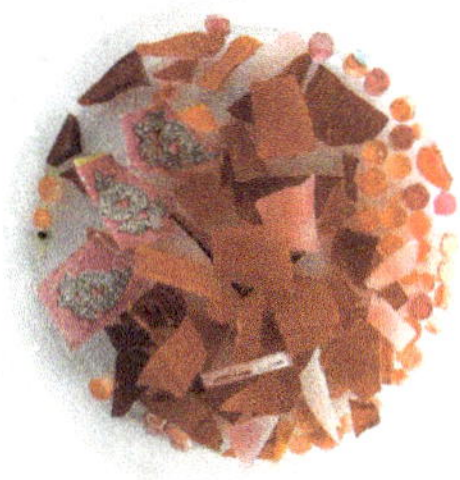

9 Paste the shards around the frame. If the hamsa has holes for hanging like in the one I used, make sure not to paste over them.

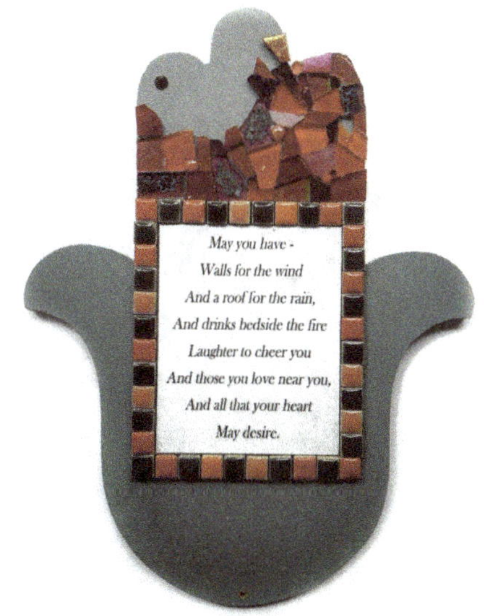

10 Let it dry for a day, then prepare dark-gray grout according to manufacturer instructions.

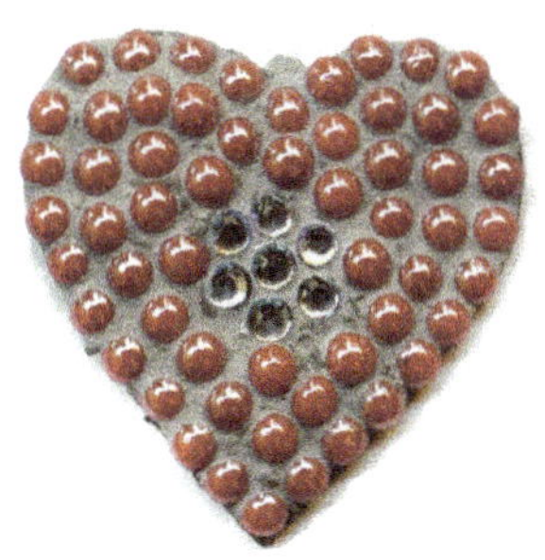

11 Consider adding various decorative elements below the hamsa (arrange for an adequately sized hole at the bottom).

12 Add a hanger and enjoy a hamsa with something to say!

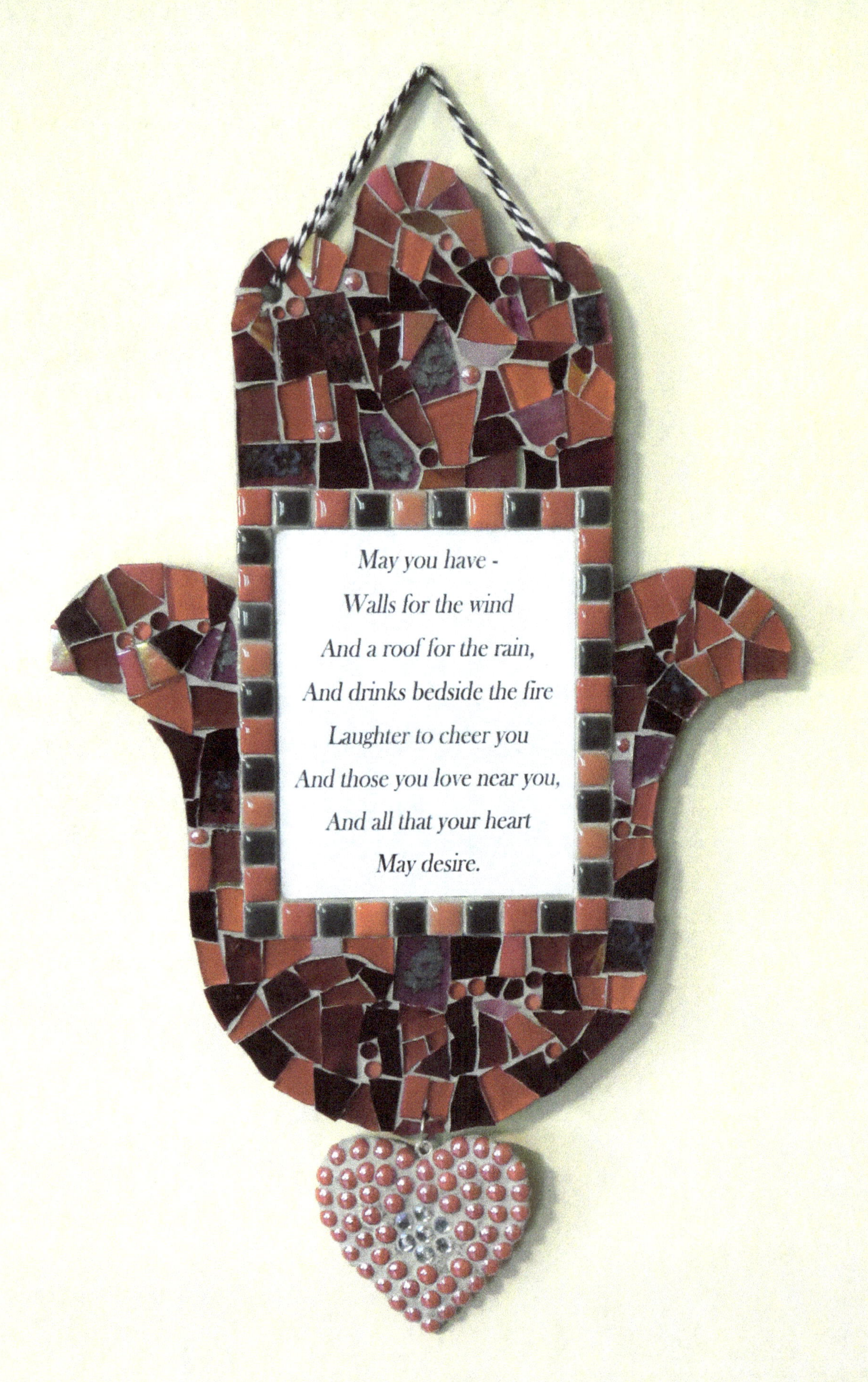

May you have -
Walls for the wind
And a roof for the rain,
And drinks bedside the fire
Laughter to cheer you
And those you love near you,
And all that your heart
May desire.

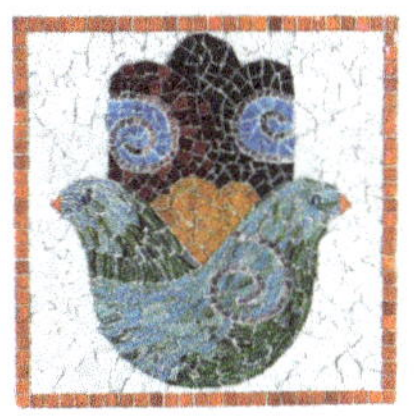

Project No. 6: Bird Hamsa

I'm very fond of birds and find myself incorporating them into many mosaic pieces. This hamsa picture depicts two birds facing in opposite directions. The glass cutting in the birds' bodies is performed so there's a feeling of movement and flow.

The work itself is made of glass and ceramic squares, mirrors and cut glass. You can craft it to any size and even if you don't want to create it as a hamsa, you can use this technique for creating just the birds.

Materials:

A wooden board measuring 40 x 40 cm / 15.7" x 15.7"
Glass tiles in shades of red, orange, dark and light green, light blue and turquoise
Orange glass tiles measuring 1.5 x 1.5 cm / 0.6" x 0.6"
White glass
2 blue beads
PVA white glue

Paintbrush
Wheeled glass nipper
Tiles cutter
Glass cutter
T-ruler
Running plier
Green Grout
Grout gear: Mixing bowl, water, a wooden stick, rags, gloves

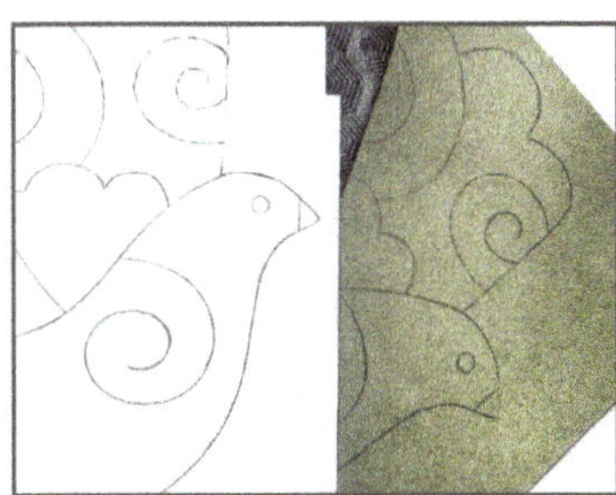

1 Copy the hamsa pattern to the wooden board using tracing paper.

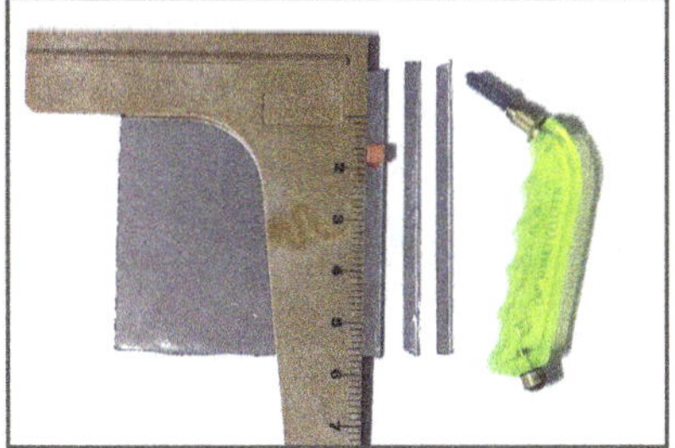

2 Begin with the three spirals: First, cut the mirror into uniform-width strips. See detailed instructions on page 27.

3 Using the nipper, cut the strips into small rectangles. Try to occasionally cut the tip of the rectangle diagonally so that the shards connect to one another accurately during rotation.

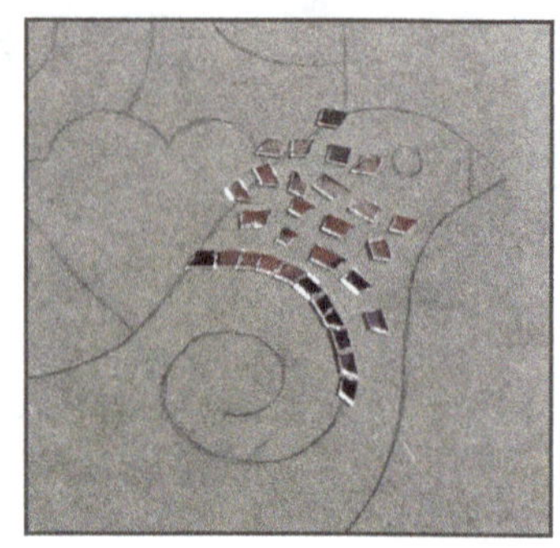

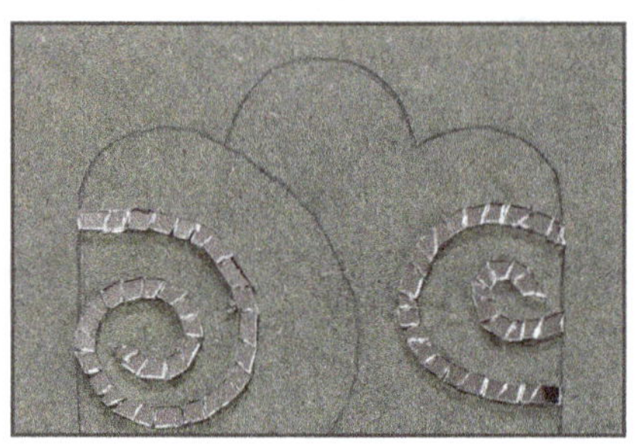

4 Paste the two remaining spirals using the same technique.

5 Cut the bird body with the nipper out of square tiles in shades of azure and green. The cutting method is as follows:

Hold the square diagonally, pointy tip downward. First, cut a triangle at the end. Then, continue cutting thin strips lengthwise. You should get long shapes, often with pointy tips, not always uniform (but that's okay), since the nipper's wheels don't always cut straight.

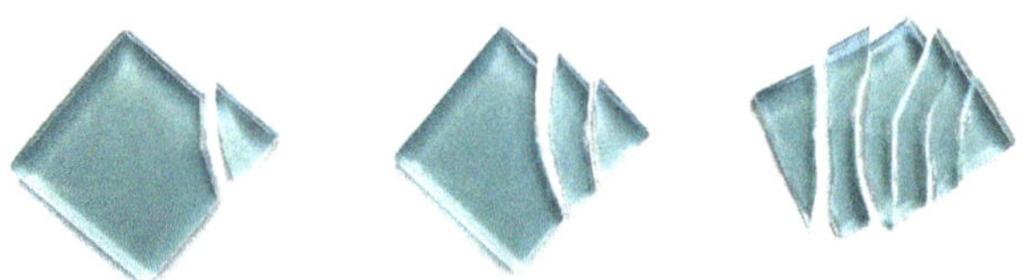

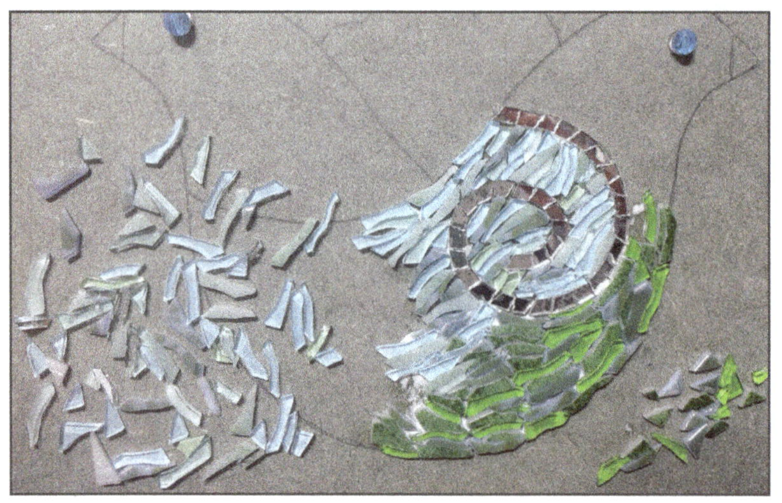

6 Paste the green shades at the bottom of the bird, while maintaining a constant direction. All shards must be glued in the same flow to create the feeling of movement.

7 Cut an orange square into two triangles, for bird beaks.

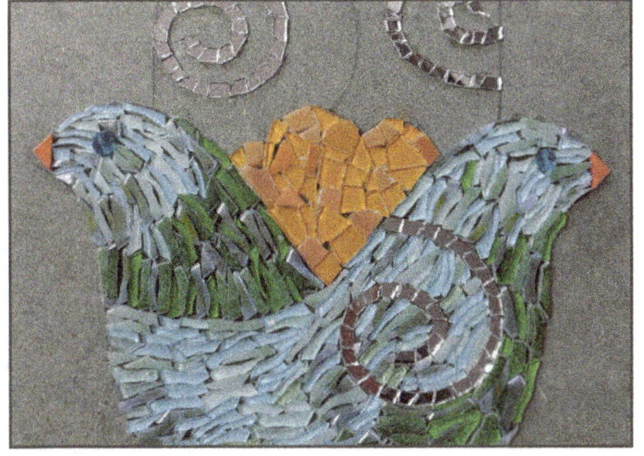

8 Finish the two birds with this method. You can mix different shades of azure and green. Paste blue glass beads for eyes.

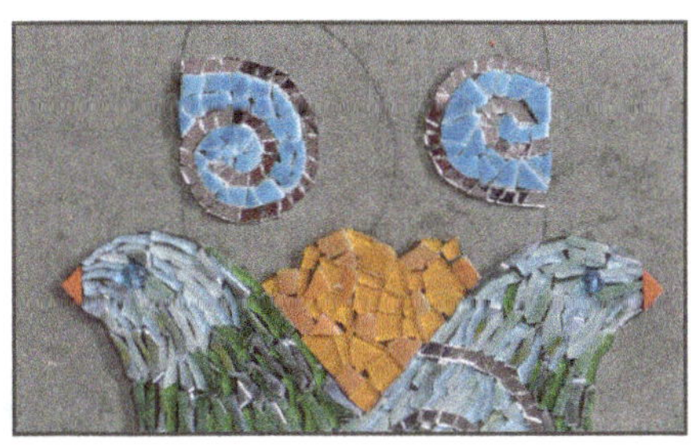

9 Cut the orange glass squares into random shapes and paste above the birds.

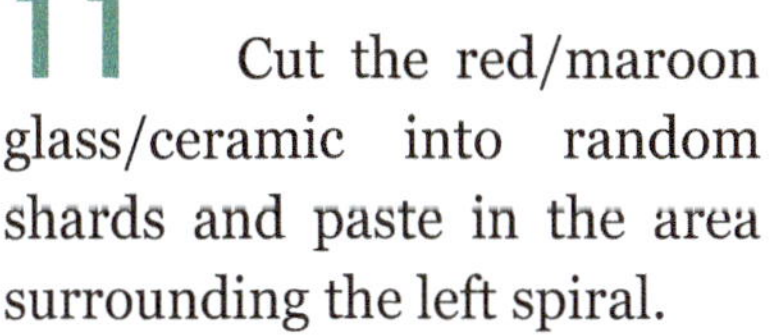

10 Cut the turquoise squares into shards that will fit the inside of the upper spirals and paste tightly together.

11 Cut the red/maroon glass/ceramic into random shards and paste in the area surrounding the left spiral.

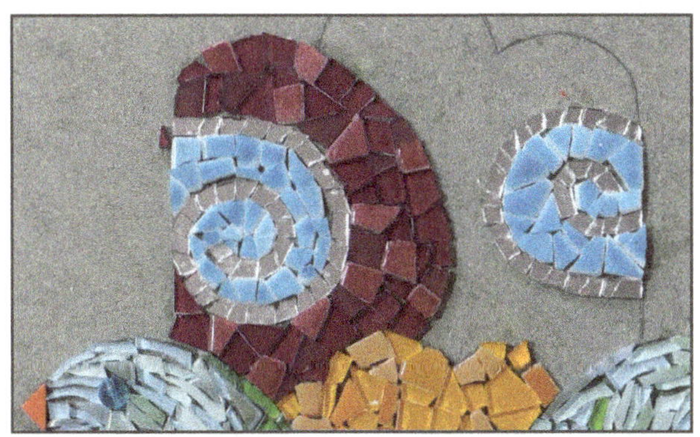

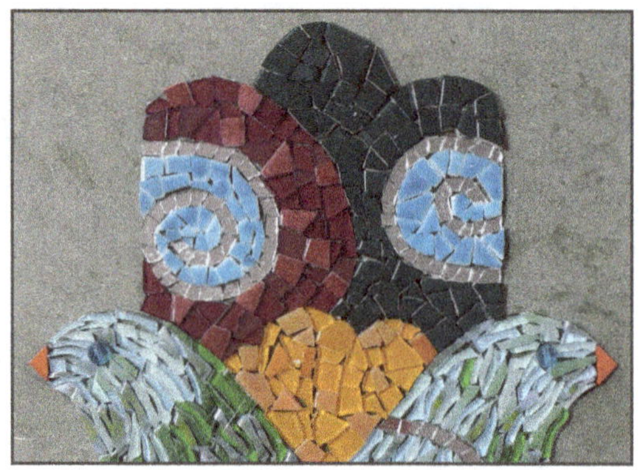

12 Cut green tiles and finish the upper right side of the hamsa.

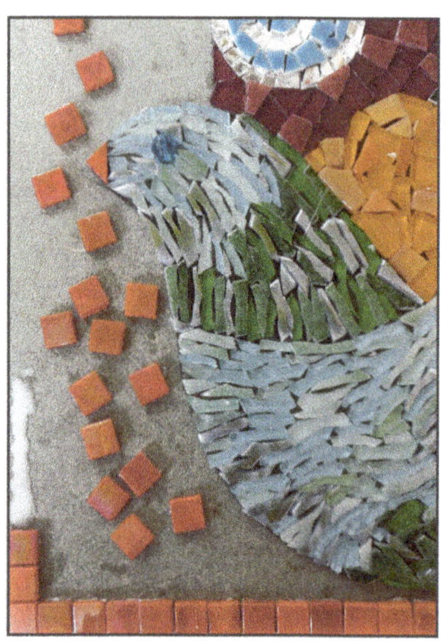

13 Assemble the frame with orange squares. Keep the pasting as straight as you can.

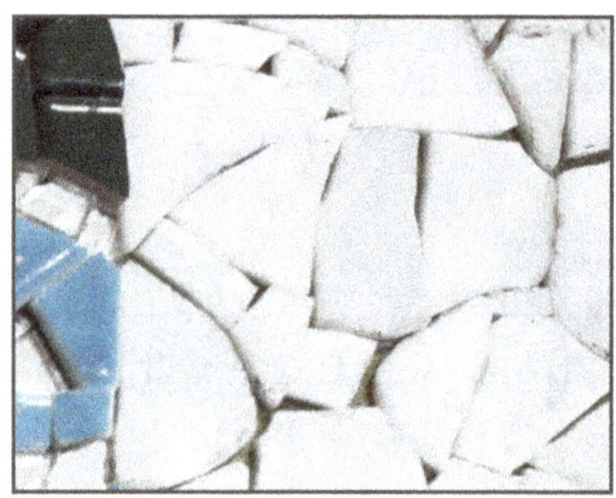

14 In the hamsa's backdrop, glue white glass that you've cut into random shards.

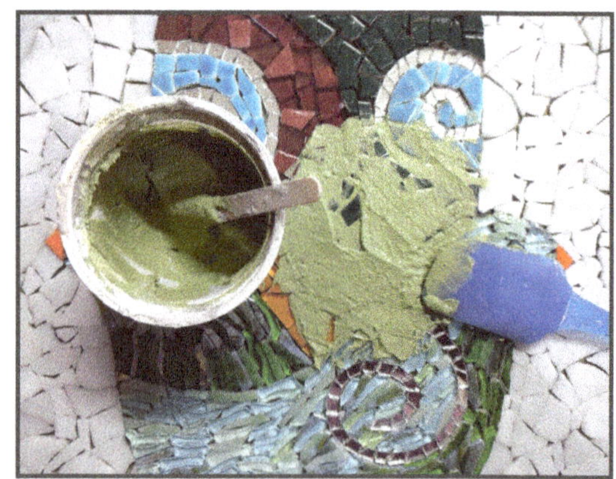

15 Leave to dry for one day, and prepare green grout according to manufacturer instructions. To achieve the light-green shade, add some acrylic paint to white grout until satisfied.

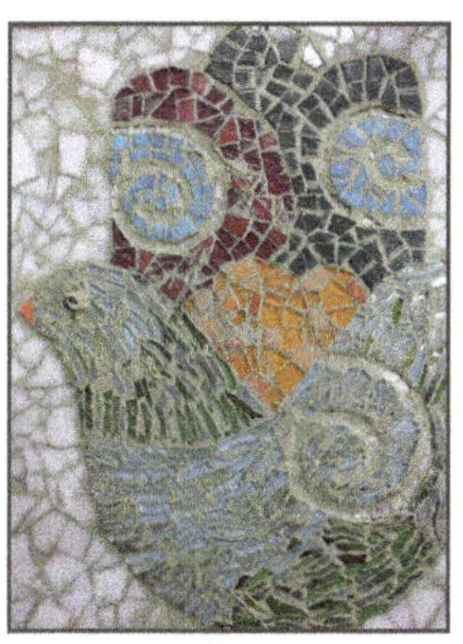

16 Apply the grout so that it would fill all the crevices, clean with a wet rag or sponge thoroughly.

17 All done! Fit a suitable hanger and enjoy your handiwork! It might be a bit heavy, so consider having a professional add the hanger.

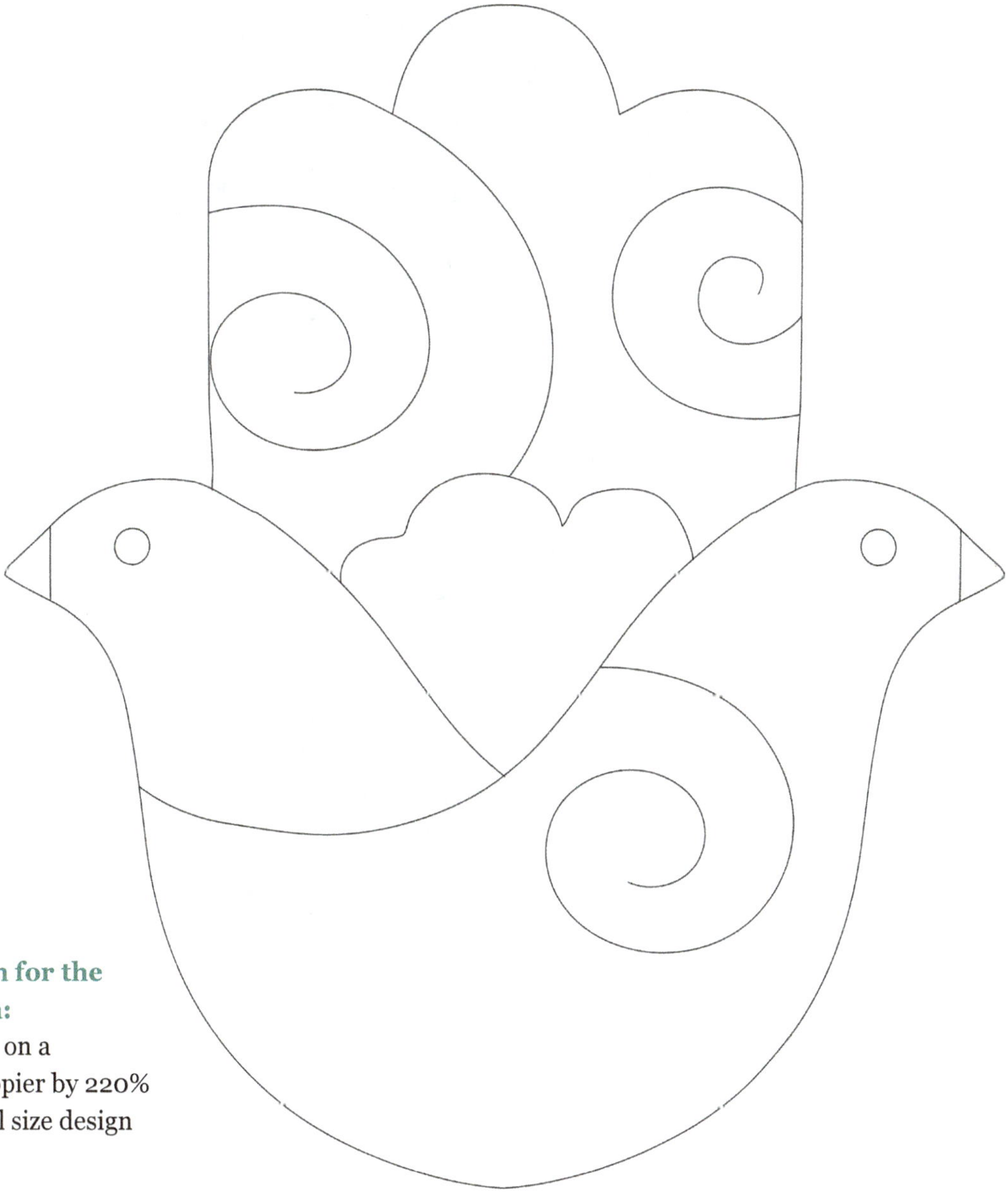

Pattern for the Hamsa:
Enlarge on a photocopier by 220% for a full size design

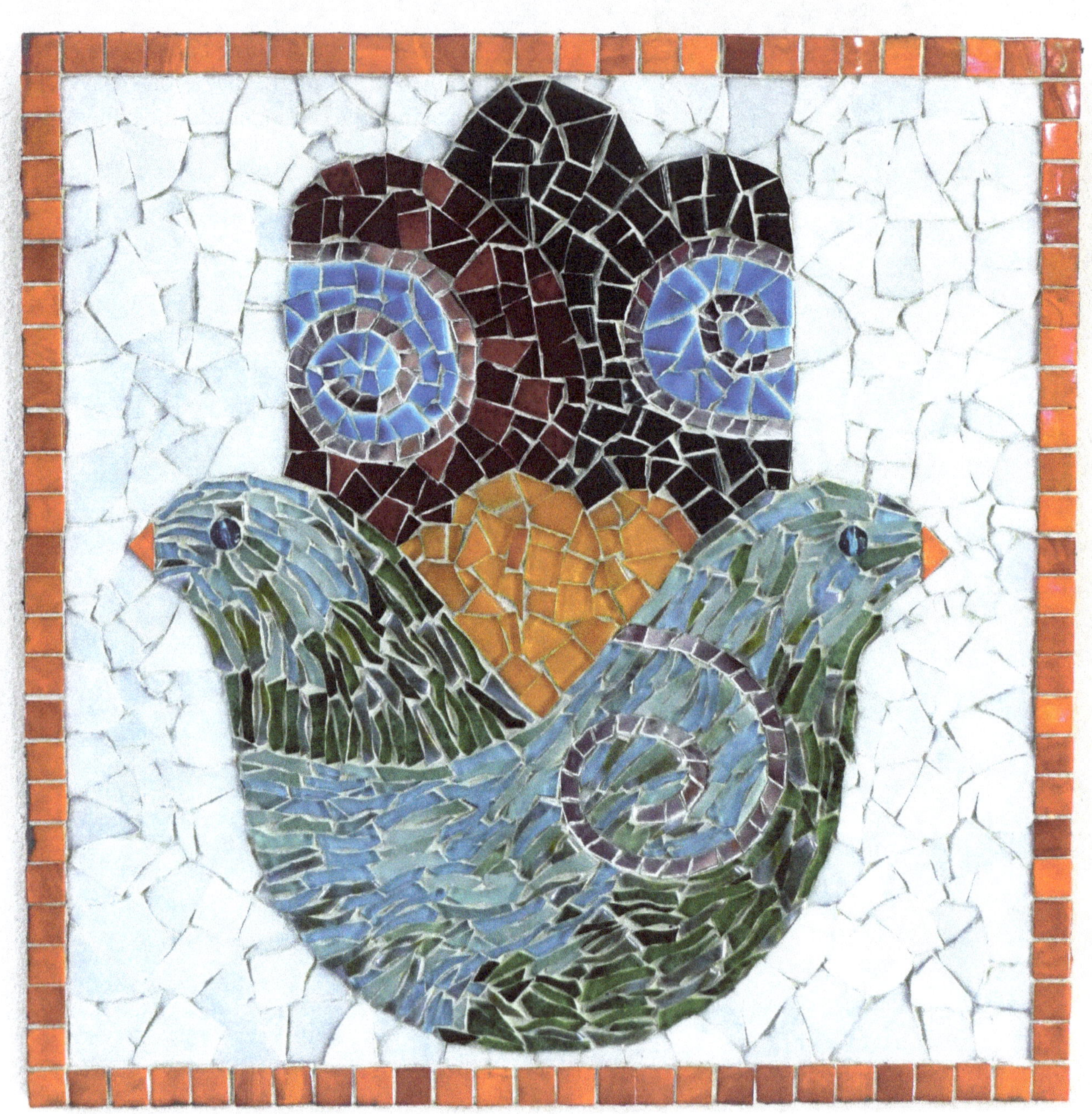

Before cutting, put on safety goggles to protect your eyes from small fragments.

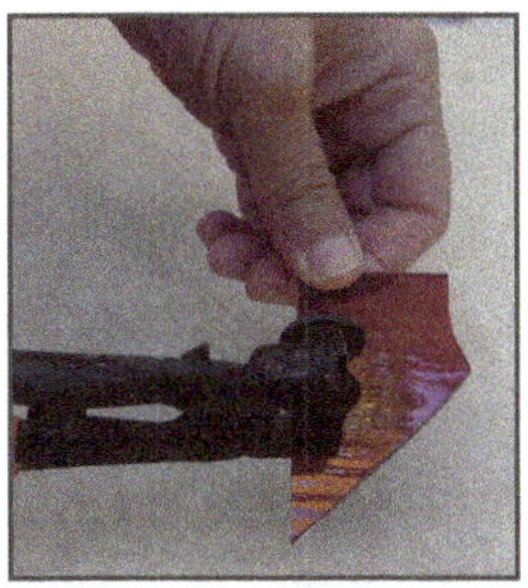

Hold the glass nipper with your dominant hand by its bottom element. Use your other hand to hold the glass. Place the glass between the wheels and cut away. The shape you'll get depends on the angle and manner in which you hold the glass. Over time, you'll learn to control the nipper grip and succeed in creating whatever shape you like.

Tip: When cutting glass, tiny pieces could shoot off in any direction. It's a good idea to cut inside a deep bowl (a plastic box would also do). You'd be wise to use gloves to avoid scrapes and cuts.

In order to cut a triangle shape, hold the nipper in an angle and cut to the desired shape.

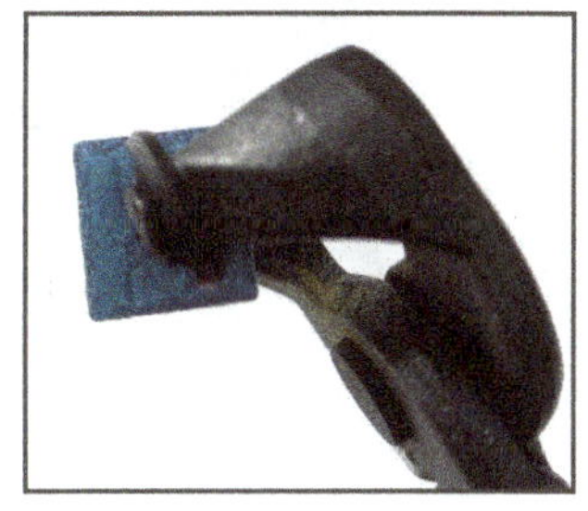

Cutting Glass Tiles

In order to cut the glass tiles, we'll use a nipper. Hold the instrument in your dominant hand and grab the glass tile at its center. Pay attention to the instrument's angle relative to the tile. The cut will follow the angle you hold it in – either straight or diagonal.

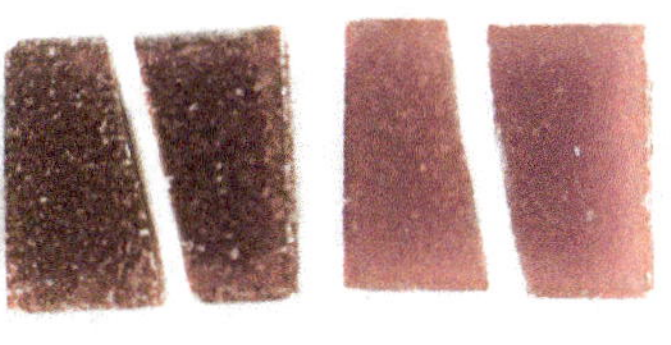

Diagonal cuts are used for creating circular patterns, making the spaces between the pieces smaller.

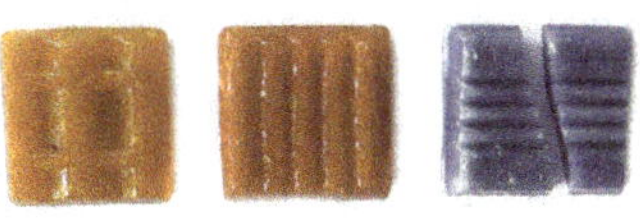

Notice the other side of the tile – It's usually rough in order to give the glue more traction. Try to cut perpendicular to the ribbing – otherwise, the cut will follow one of the ribs, making it harder to control the width of the cut.

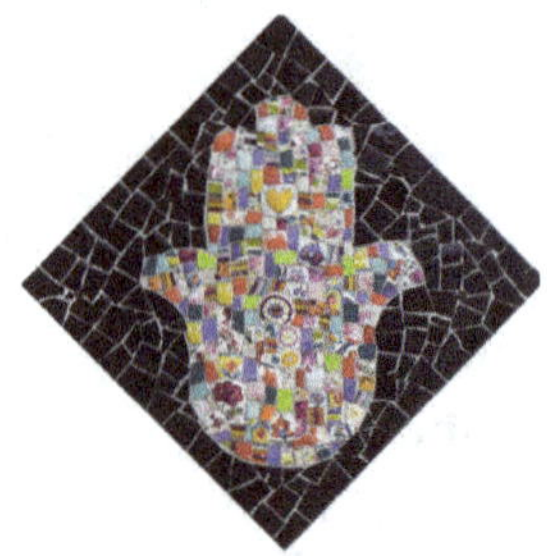

Project No. 7: Crockery Shard Hamsa on Tile

With the huge conversation going on around recycling, it's high time that we do a little repurposing of ourselves. That is what our next hamsa is all about.

I love using broken crockery for my mosaics. I have shelves chock-full of colorful pieces brought over by friends and neighbors. They all know not to throw out anything that's cracked or broken, and bring it to me instead. Win-win all around.

This hamsa is composed from shards of colorful plates and glasses I've collected, and is built on a square tile that you can hang outdoors. Naturally, you can choose any other suitable base, with regard to the correct type of glue.

To highlight the colors' flamboyance, the hamsa will be surrounded by cut black tiles.

Materials:

Thick ceramic tile measuring 30x30cm/11.8x11.8"
Colorful crockery shards cut into squares
Black tile shards
Wheeled glass nipper

Wooden stick
Tile adhesive
Dark gray grout
Grout gear: Mixing bowl, water, a wooden stick, rags, gloves

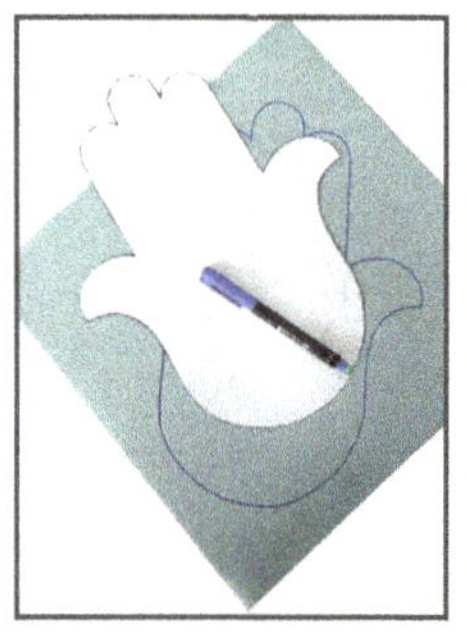

1 Cut out the hamsa and trace it onto a square tile using a suitable marker.

2 Prepare plates and cups of various colors and patterns. First, cut them into large random pieces. See instructions for cutting colorful crockery using the nipper on page 54.

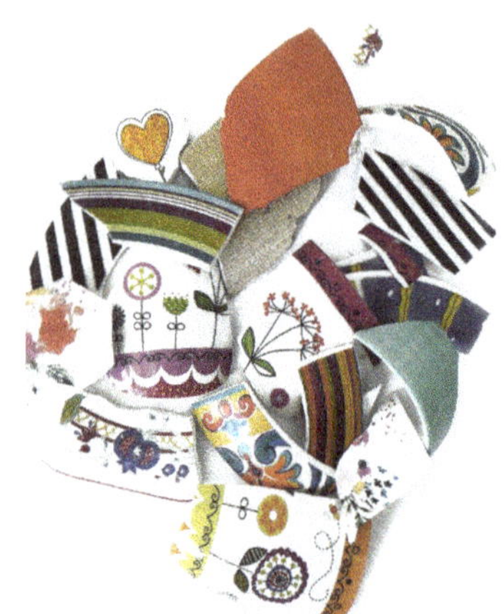

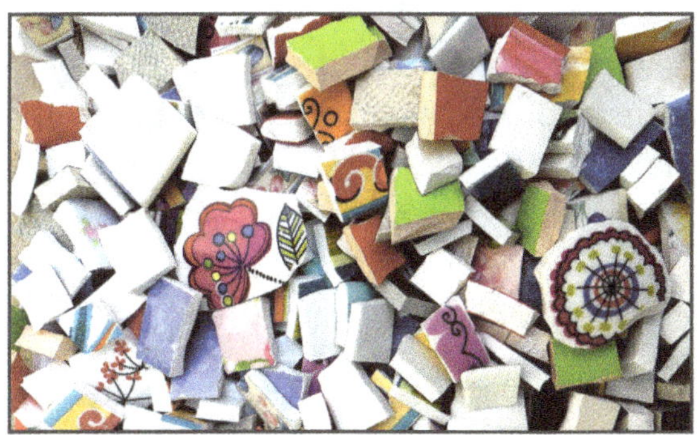

3 Cut the crockery into small rectangular shards, as well as some triangular ones. If the pieces have circular patterns, you can cut around them to highlight the circles.

4 Using tile glue, paste the colorful shards to the shape of the hamsa. Start at the bottom and keep the contour as accurate as possible.

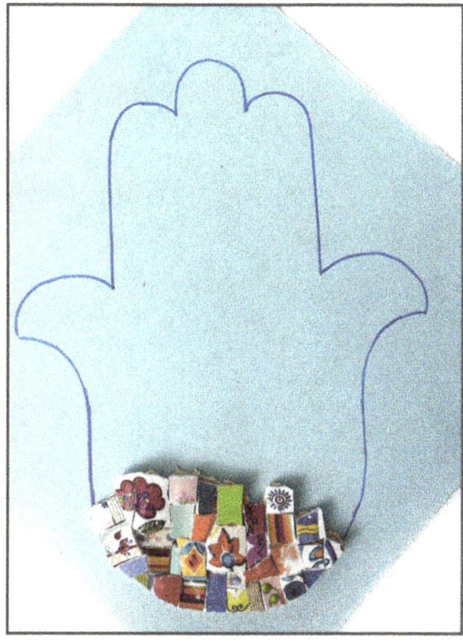

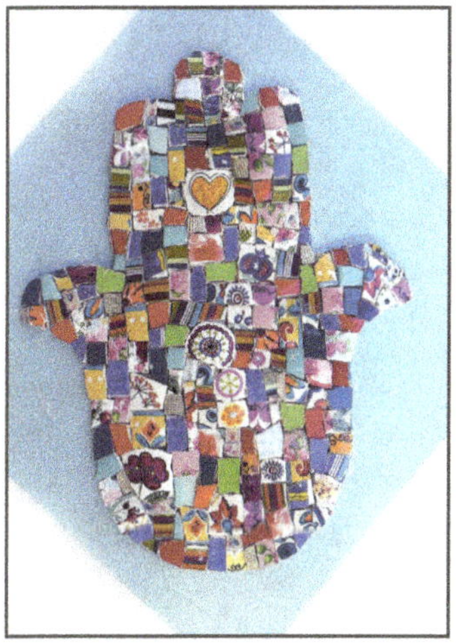

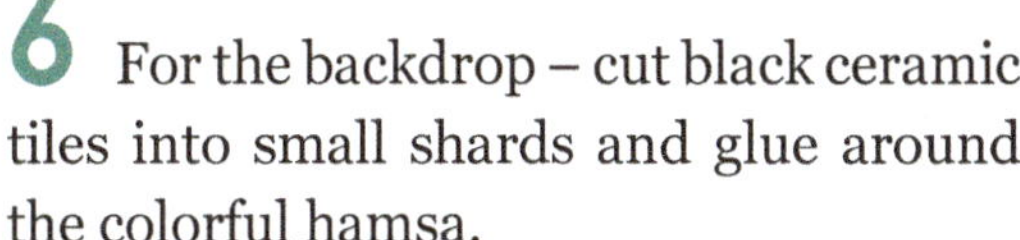

5 Complete the hamsa using the same method. You can incorporate circular shapes or floral patterns among the rectangular shards.

6 For the backdrop – cut black ceramic tiles into small shards and glue around the colorful hamsa.

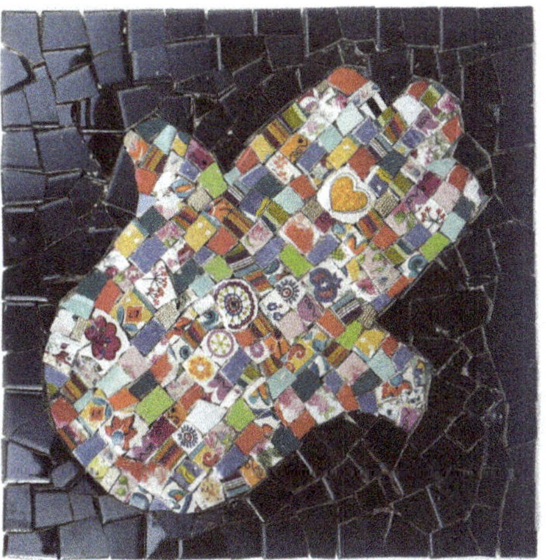

7 Let it dry for a day and prepare dark-gray grout according to manufacturer instructions. Apply it to the tile with a spatula, and make sure the grout reaches every crevice since the surface has varying heights (not all cut shards are the same height, which is fine).

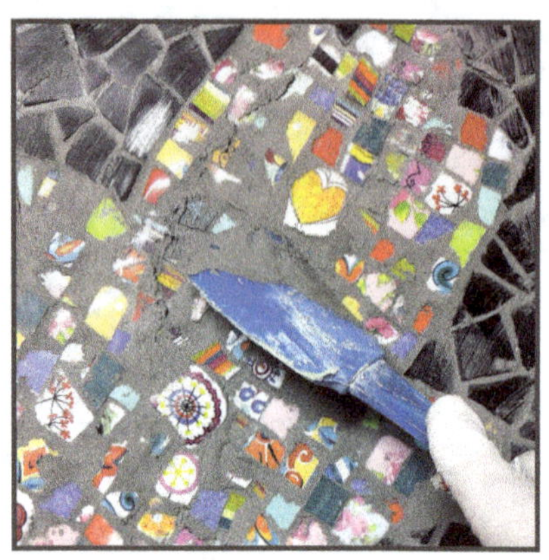

8 Clean thoroughly with a wet sponge or rag. Glue to the wall with tile glue or a strong acrylic glue.

Tip: If the tile is heavy, first attach a wooden board to the wall as support, and glue the tile onto it so that it won't slip. Roughly an hour after the glue has dried, make sure the tile is secure and remove the board.

Pattern for the Hamsa:
Enlarge on a photocopier by 200% for a full size design

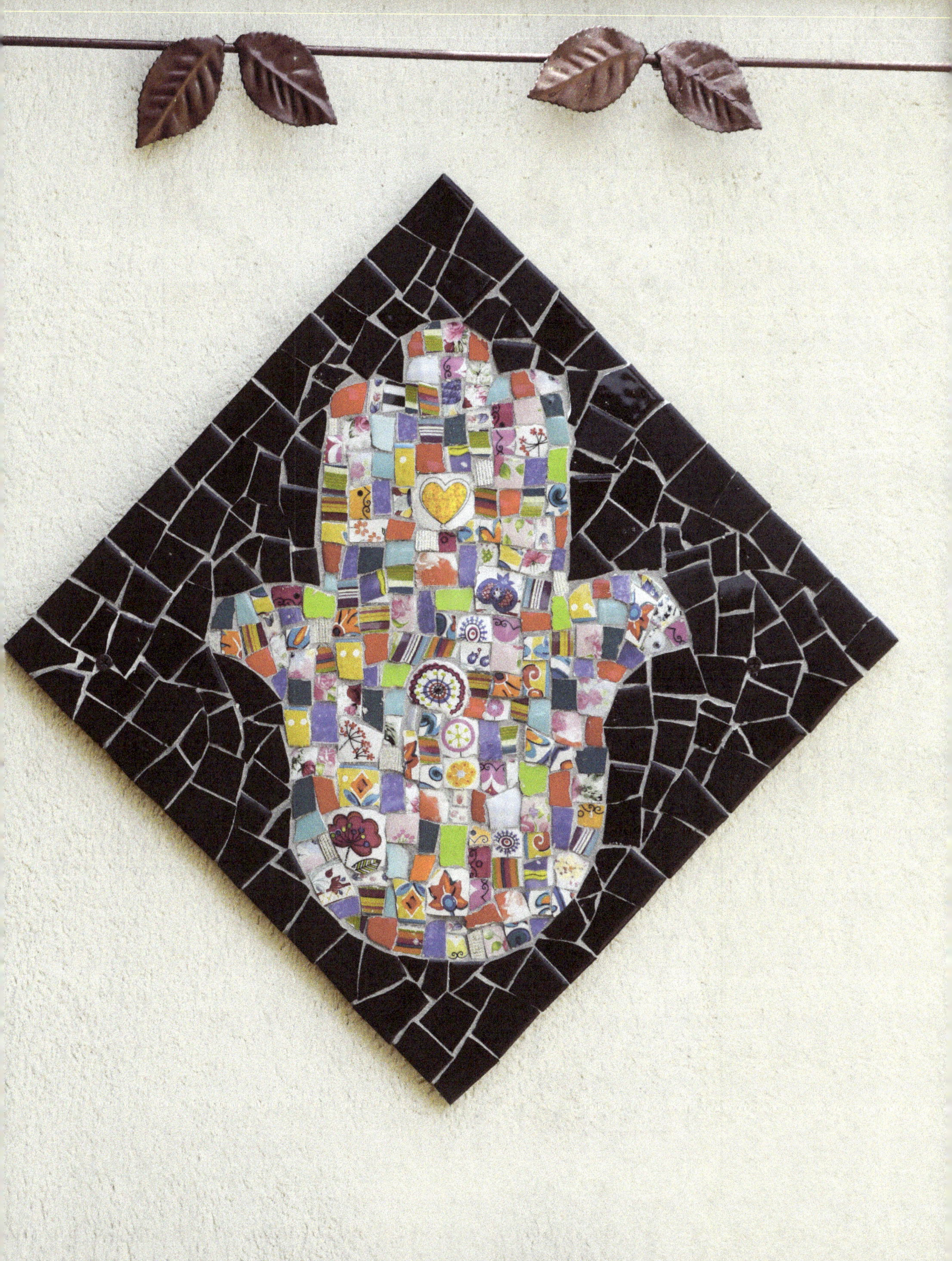

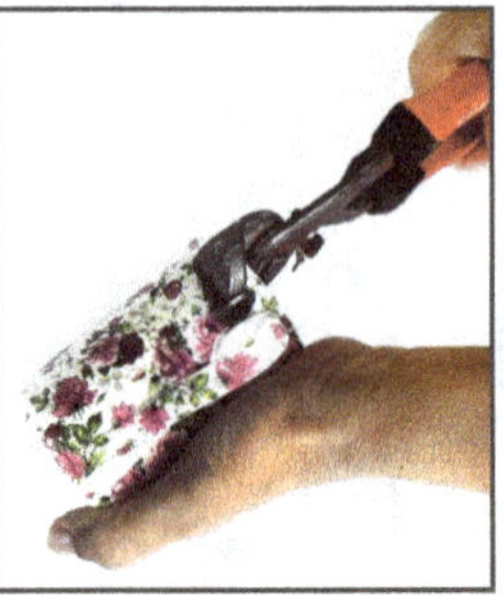

1 Hold the nipper with your dominant hand, and support the piece with your other hand. Bring the nipper to the rim, with the wheels clutching it from both sides.

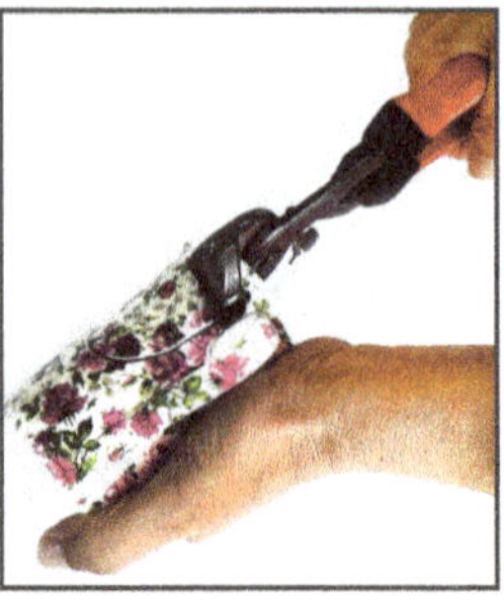

2 Firmly press the nipper until the piece is cut.

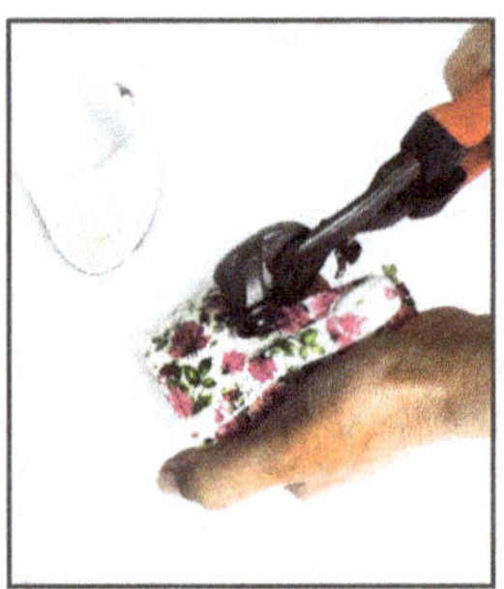

3 Continue in the same direction until the piece is cut in two.

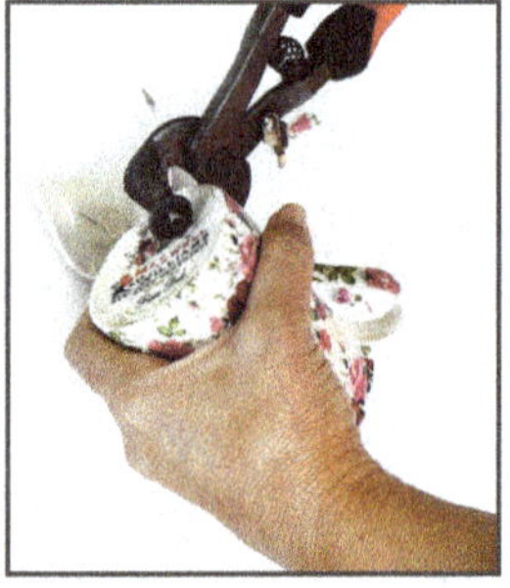

4 Use additional cuts to remove the excess pieces (like the bottom of a cup).

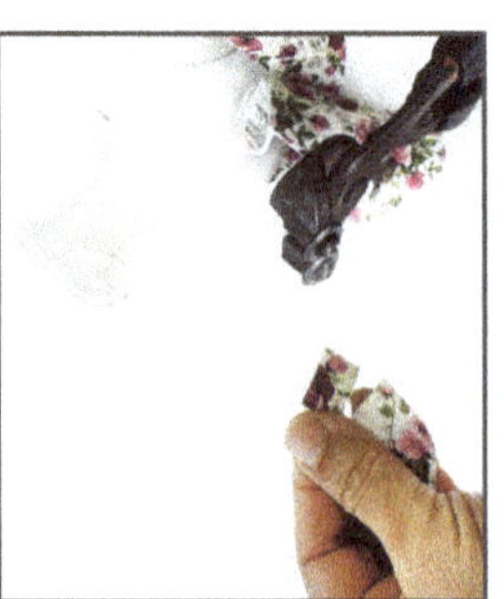

5 Now, cut the shards to the size and shape you desire.

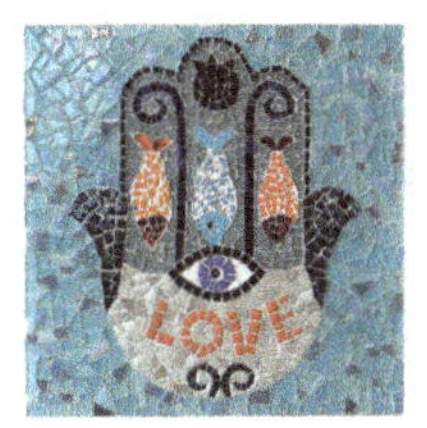

Project No. 8: Hamsa Picture Frame with Traditional Elements and Two-Tone Grout

Traditional hamsas are meant to guard against the evil eye, protect the home and bless those living in it. In this hamsa, I chose to incorporate various elements of opulence and blessing: The eye, which guards against the evil eye; three fish, a symbol of wealth and prosperity, blessings and productivity, made from broken crockery and glass in different shades; a red pomegranate, symbol of wealth and spirituality (according to Jewish tradition, it holds 613 seeds, the number of mitzvahs), and the inscription "Love" – And what more do we need?

For the hamsa's finish, I used two colors of grout – gray for the hamsa itself and azure for the backdrop. The backdrop is made from different shades of azure combined with beads, and the azure grout unifies the background, highlighting the hamsa within the variety of colors.

This hamsa is suitable for hanging on a wall and can be crafted in any size you wish, with or without a backdrop.

Materials:

A wooden board measuring 40 x 40 cm / 15.7" x 15.7"

Black and Red tiles measuring 1 x 1 cm / 0.39" x 0.39"

Glass tiles in shades of blue, metal, gray, light blue and beige

A black bead for the pupil

3 small black beads for the fish eyes

Colored glass in shades of blue, azure, red and orange

Colored crockery cut into squares

PVA white glue

Paintbrush

Wheeled glass nipper

Tile cutter

Light gray and light blue grout

Masking tape

Grout gear: Mixing bowl, water, a wooden stick, rags, gloves

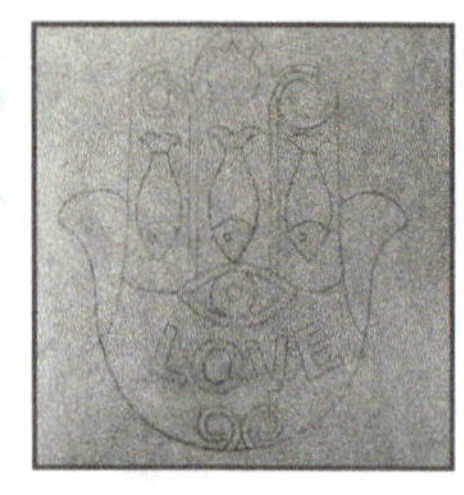

1 Copy the pattern to the wooden surface with using tracing paper.

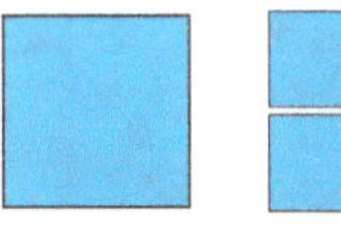 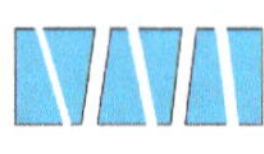

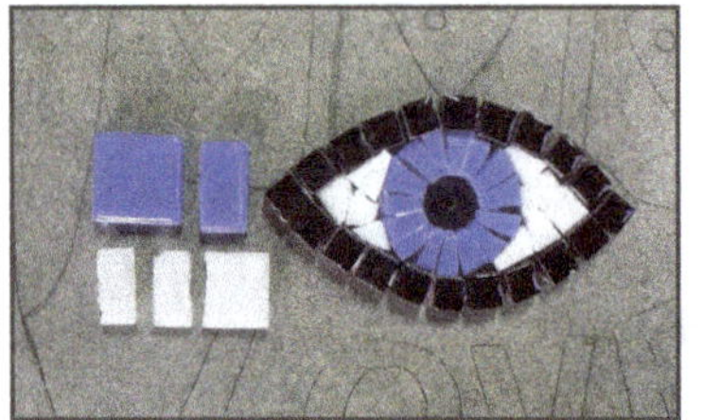

2 To craft the eye, paste a frame made of small black squares to enclose the area. Paste a round bead at the center of the pupil and blue squares around it (see cutting pattern below). Fill in the rest with white glass shards.

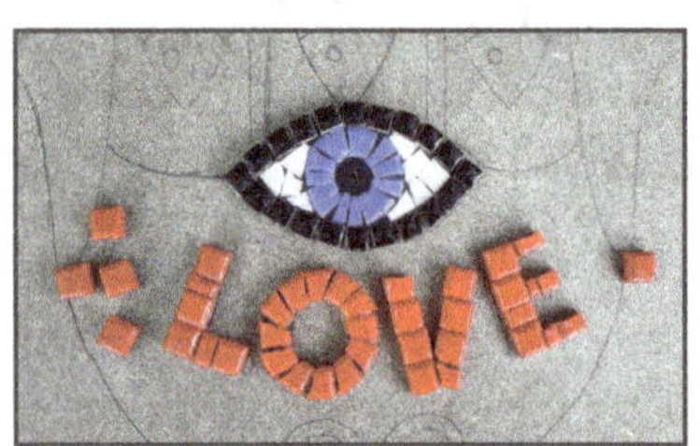

3 To make the word "LOVE" use small red squares. Cut to fit if necessary.

4 Find a cup or plate with a pattern to match the fish. For this example, I use the orange, azure and red.

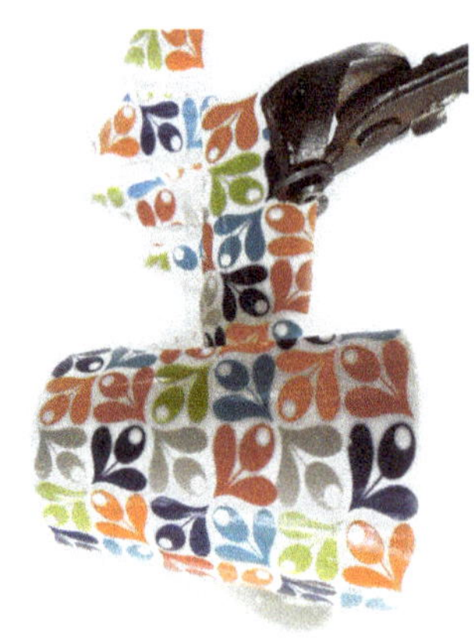

5 Cut the crockery shards into small pieces and paste on the fish bodies in a tight formation.

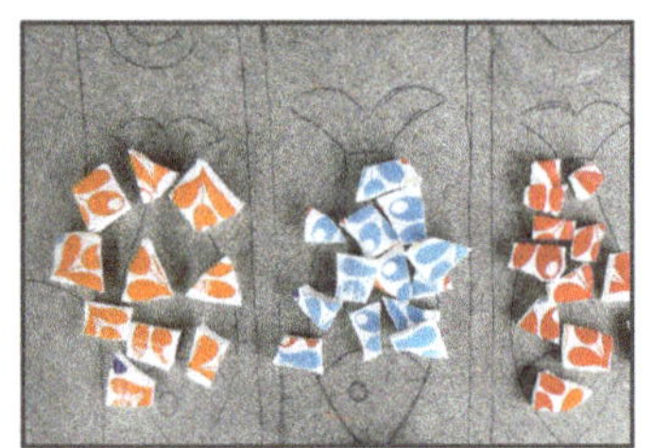

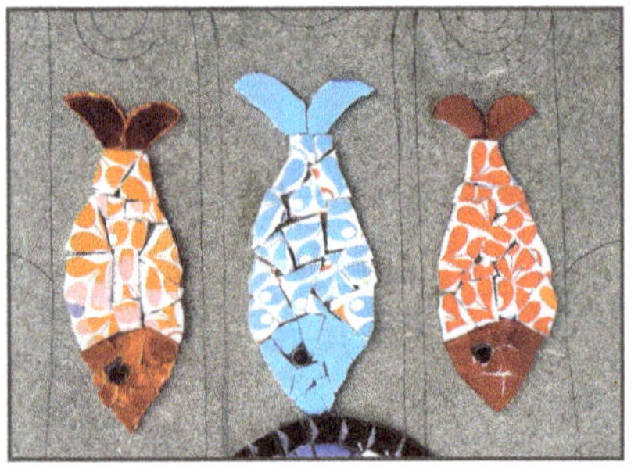

6 The fish heads and tails should be crafted from glass colored to match their bodies. Use small beads for eyes. Cut the fish tails as two separate shards pasted close together: Cut the tail pattern out of paper and trace it to the glass. Cut with a glass blade to create an accurate shape.

7 Cut strips of blue glass to create the gaps between the fingers. Cut the strips to small rectangular, square and triangular shards. See instructions for cutting glass strips on page 27.

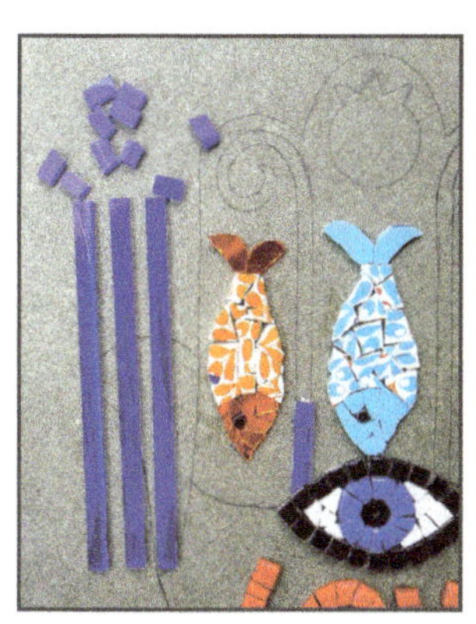

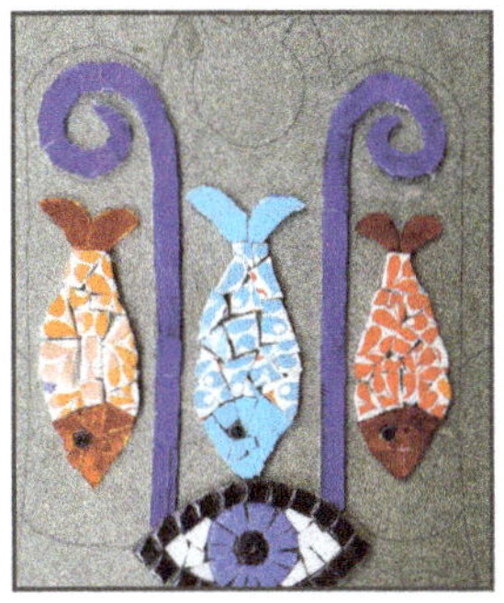

8 Paste the blue glass along the strips, as well as in the hamsa's bottom decoration. Make sure you incorporate triangles and rectangles in the rounded areas.

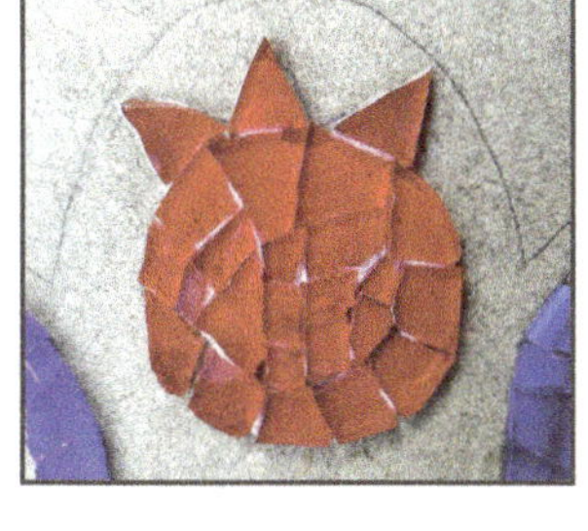

9 Cut red glass into small shards and glue the pomegranate, with three triangles at its top.

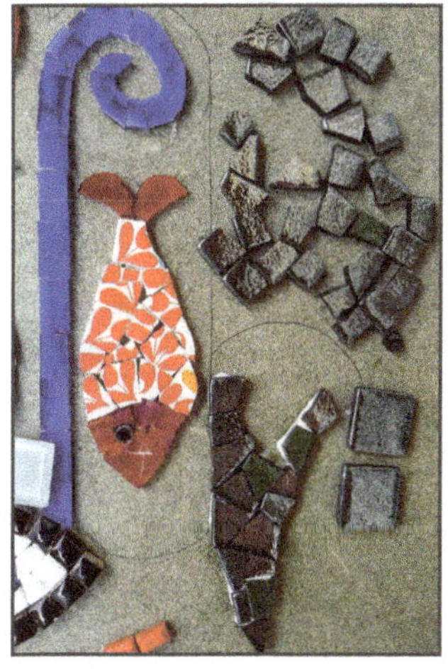

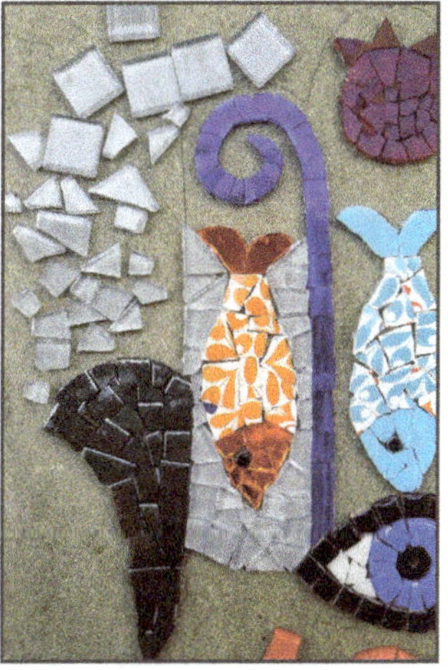

10 Cut small shards from metallic tiles for the two lateral fingers of the hamsa.

11 Cut bright-gray glass into small shards and glue the fingers' inner backdrop.

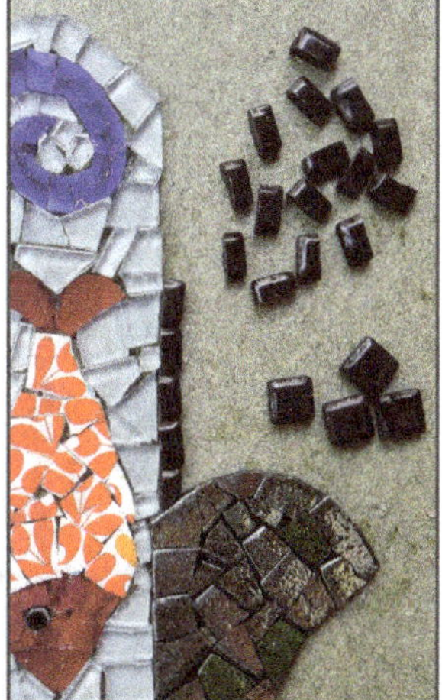

12 Around the fingers, create a black contour out of small squares cut in half. Maintain a rounded contour where necessary and cut the squares accordingly.

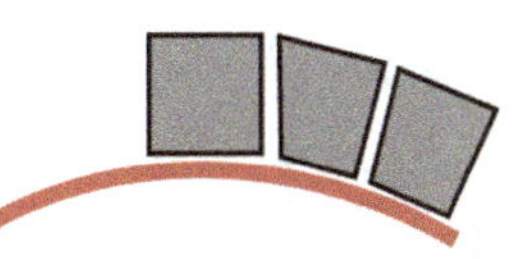

13 For pasting the bottom part, use several shades of beige glass cut into small shards.

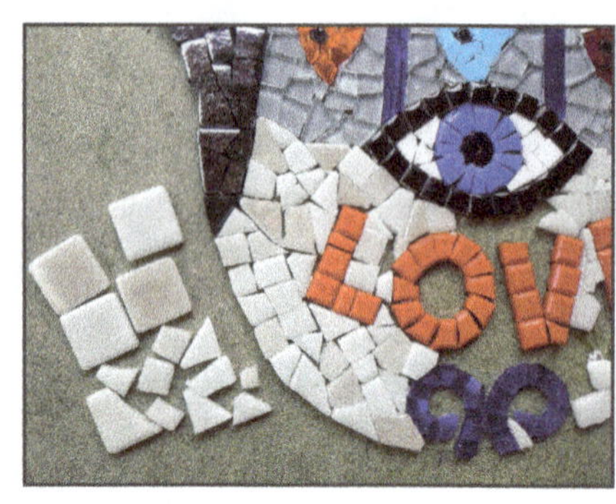

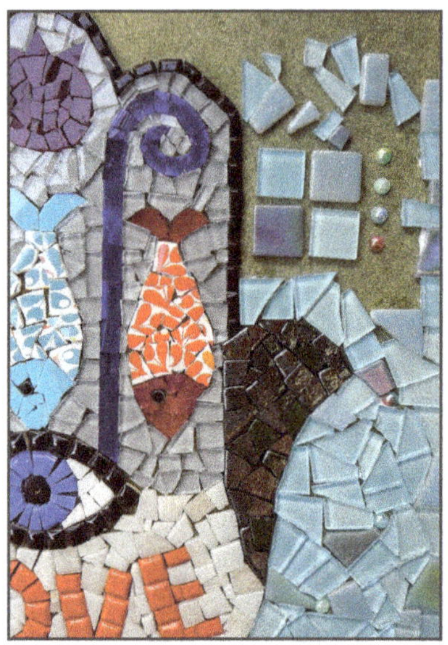

14 The hamsa backdrop should be composed of glass in shades of azure combined with round flat beads, for an interesting and diverse effect.

15 Once you're done pasting the backdrop, let dry for a day.

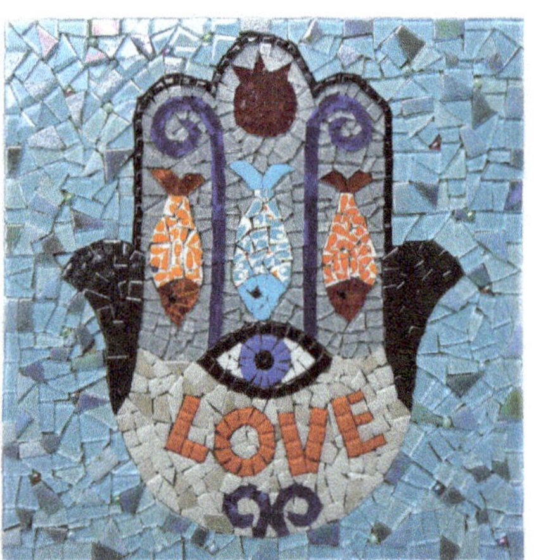

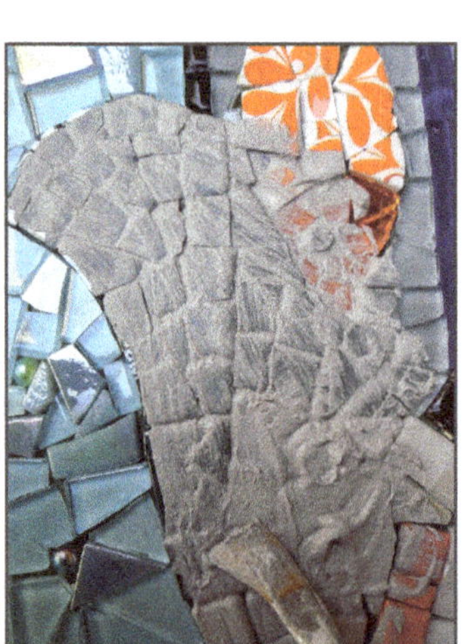

16 The grout should be applied in two stages. First, prepare light gray grout for the hamsa itself. Carefully apply with a brush while maintaining the edges clean. where necessary and cut the squares accordingly.

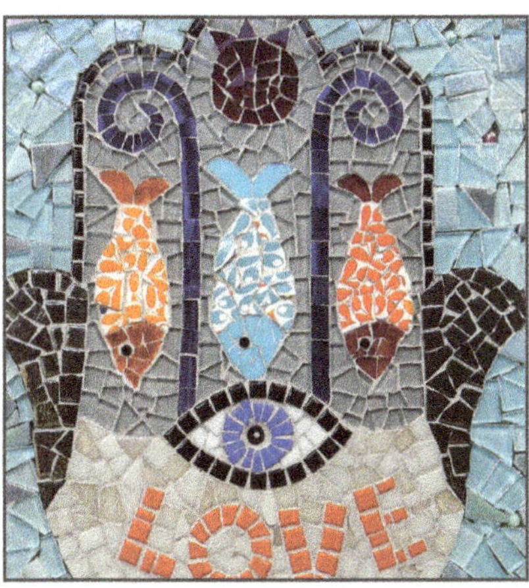

17 Clean thoroughly with wet and dry rags and wait several hours until dry – preferably for a full day.

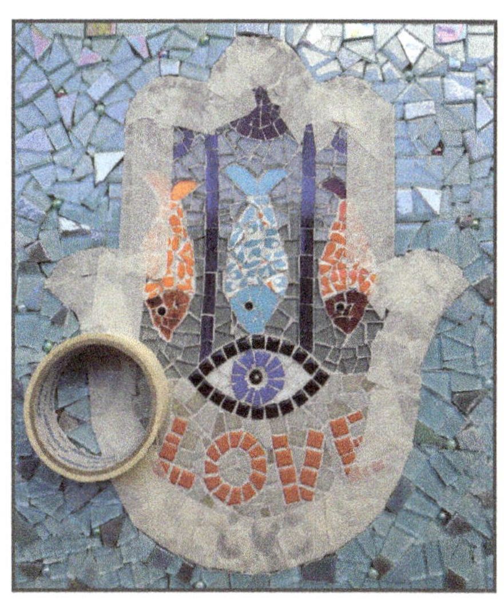

18 The azure grout is darker and can sully the bright one. To avoid that, apply masking tape to the edge of the bright area and make sure it's snug.

19 Prepare the azure grout (you can add some acrylic paint to white grout) and apply to the background. Clean carefully with wet and dry rags.

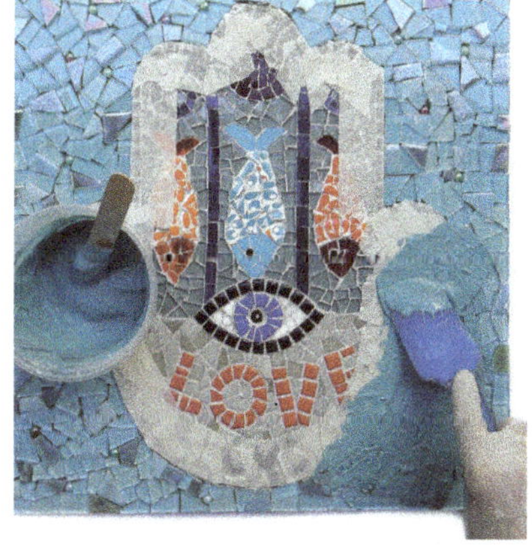

20 After the grout has dried slightly, remove the masking tape, clean up and use a brush to fill in grout where necessary.

21 All done! Attach a sturdy hanger and enjoy a beautiful, blessed hamsa!

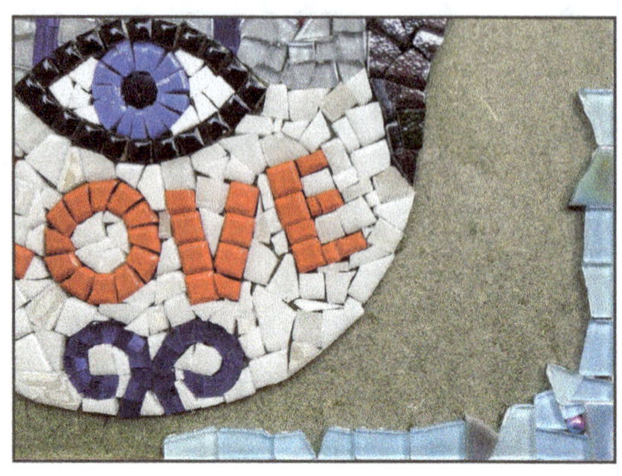

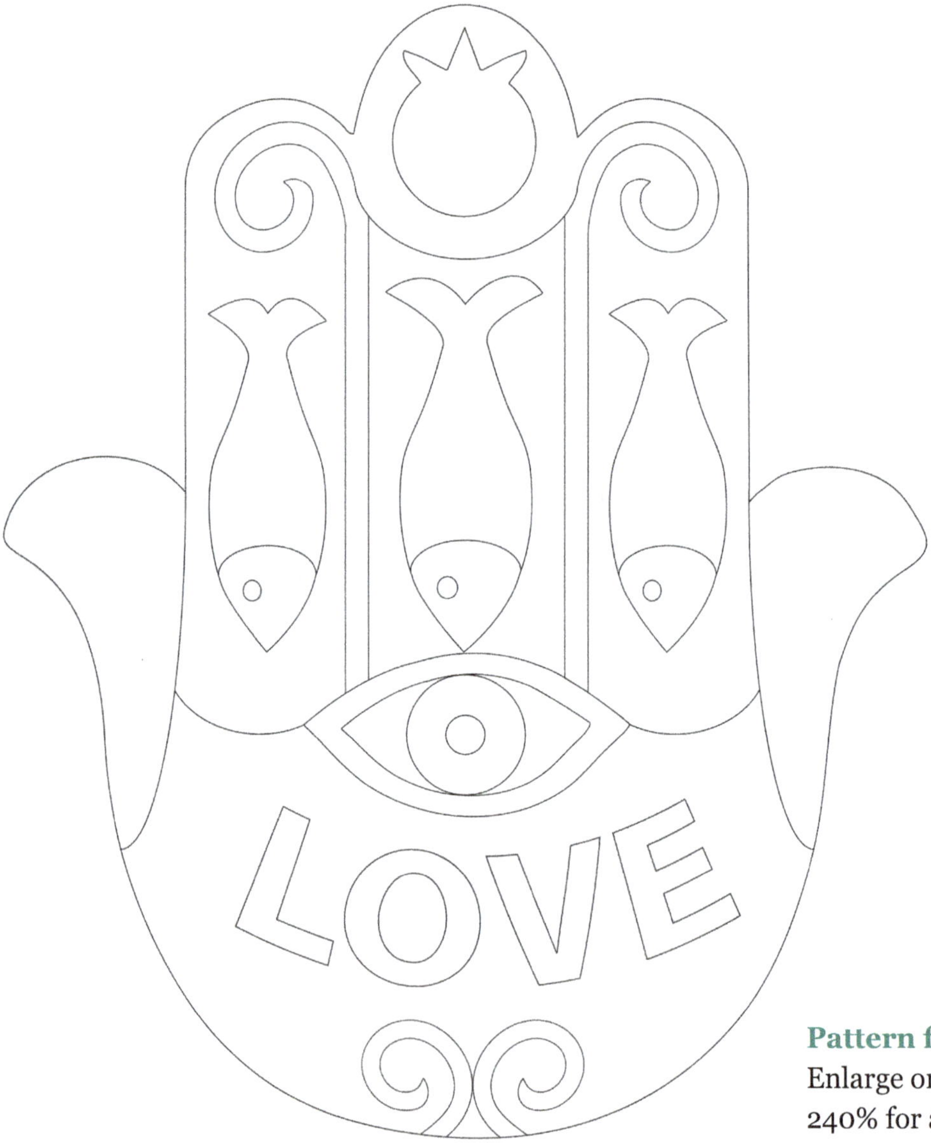

Pattern for the Hamsa:
Enlarge on a photocopier by 240% for a full size design

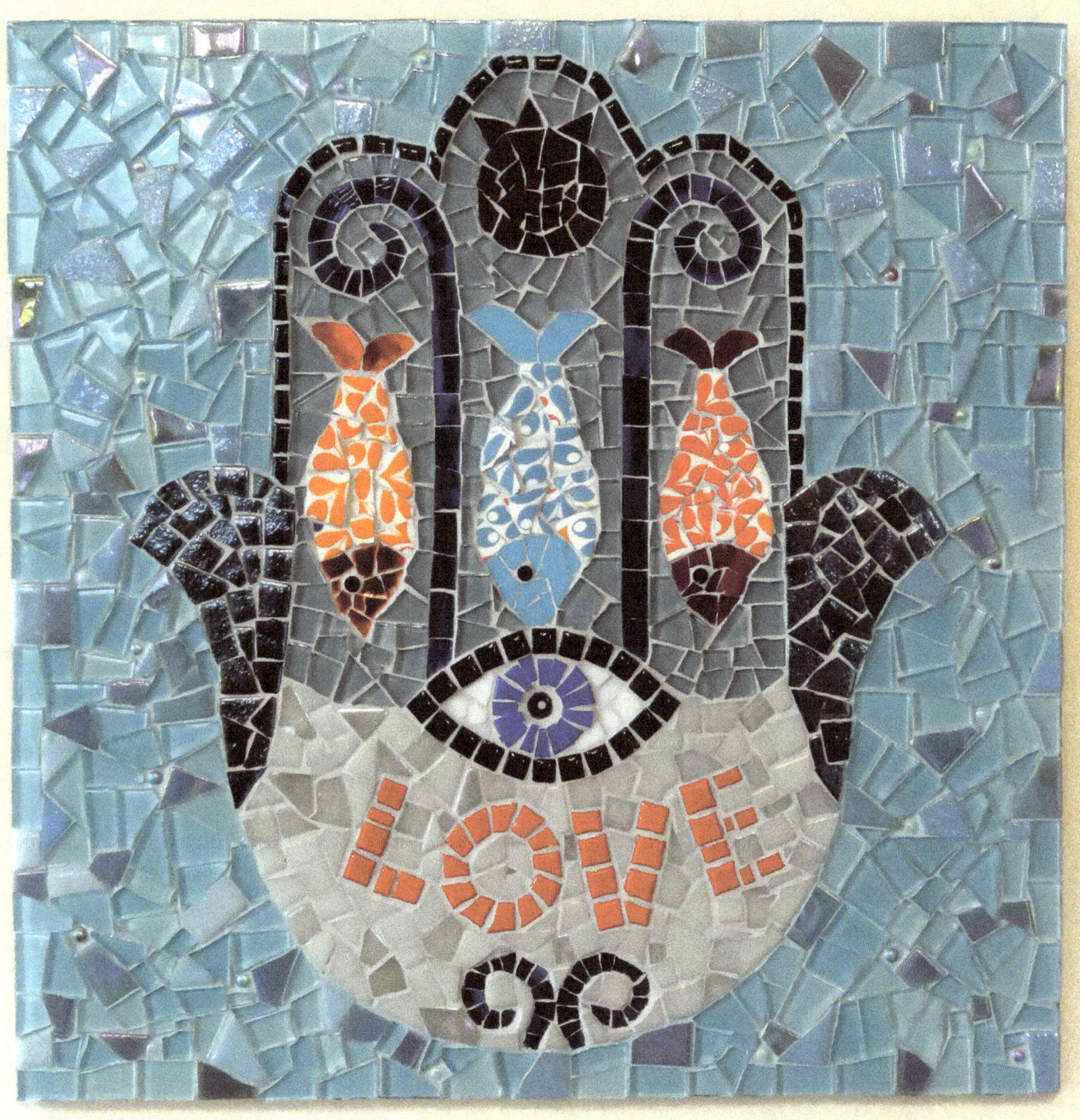

LOVE

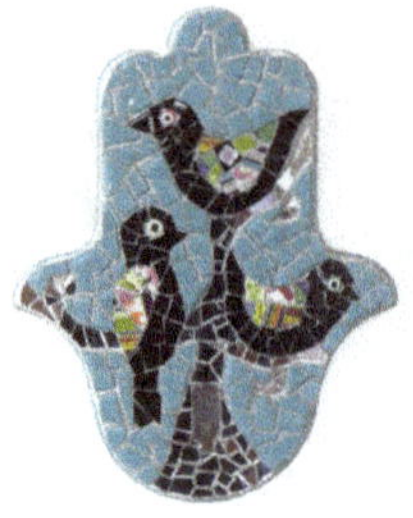

Project No. 9: Hamsa with Hanger

This hamsa is suitable for decoration but can also be useful. It can be fitted with a metal ring for hanging on a keychain, necklace or whatever comes to mind – I'm sure you'll find a good use for it.

The hanger has a shiny metal finish, so it goes well with the mirror shard-covered wood. The hamsa is decorated with three adorable birds, and can be crafted to any size desirable – with or without a hanger.

Materials:

A wooden hamsa measuring 25cm/10" in height (any other size would also do)

Mirror shards

Black glass or ceramic

Colorful crockery shards

Three round beads for eyes

Turquoise glass or ceramic for the background

Metal/silver hanger

PVA white glue

Paintbrush

Wheeled glass nipper

Gray grout

Grout gear: Mixing bowl, water, a wooden stick, rags, gloves

1 Copy the pattern onto the hamsa using tracing paper.

2 Use the nipper to cut the crockery to small shards and paste them to the birds' wings. Add an eye for each bird.

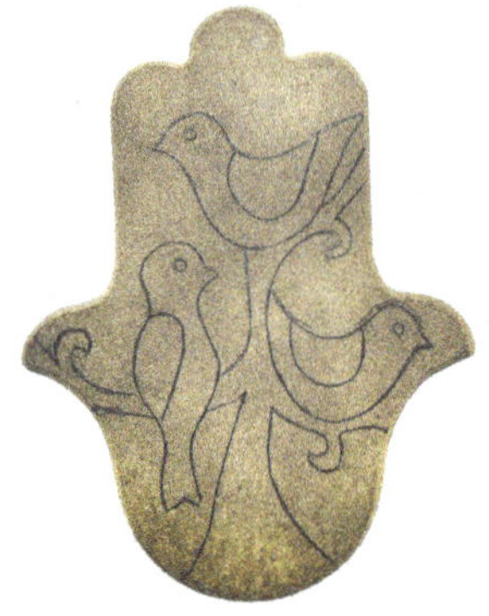

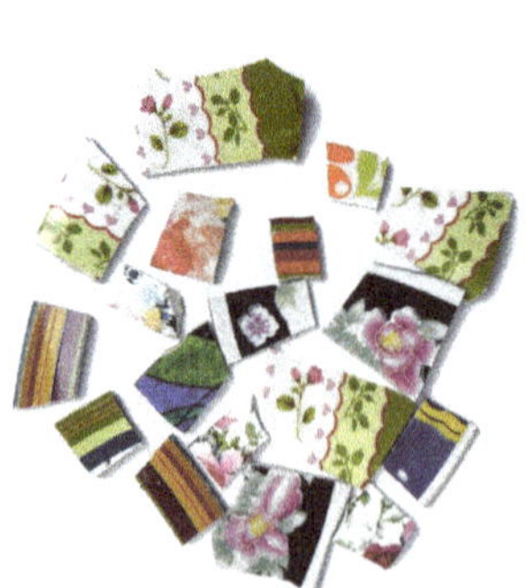

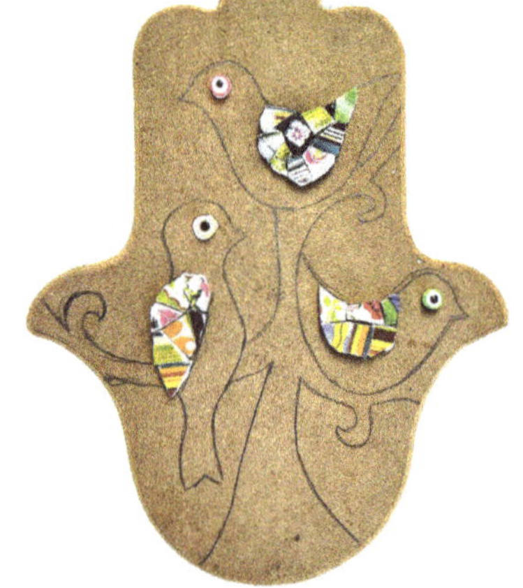

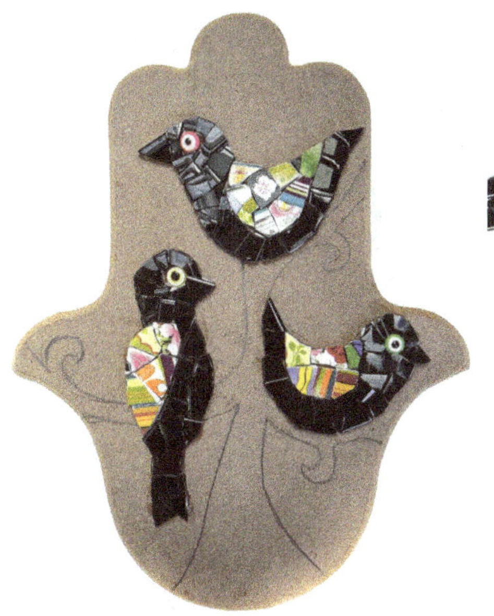

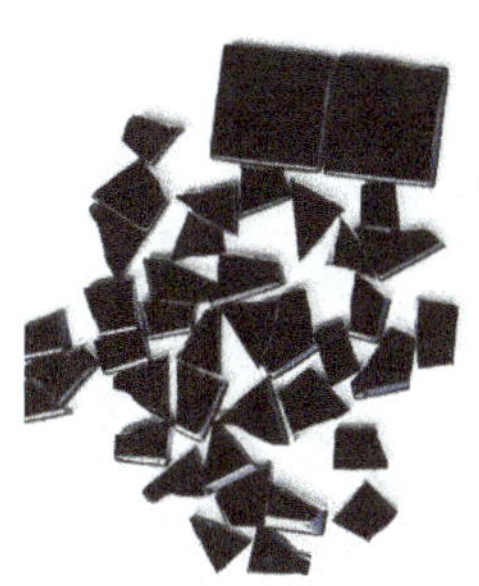

3 Cut black glass or ceramic to small shards and paste the birds' bodies.

4 Glue a silver hanger to the bottom of the hamsa.

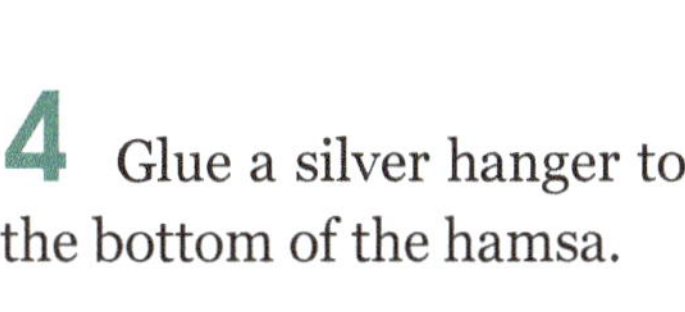

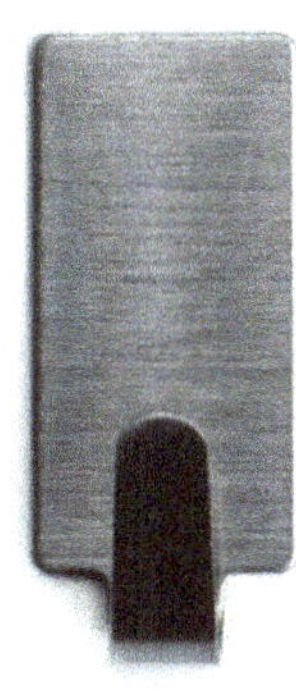

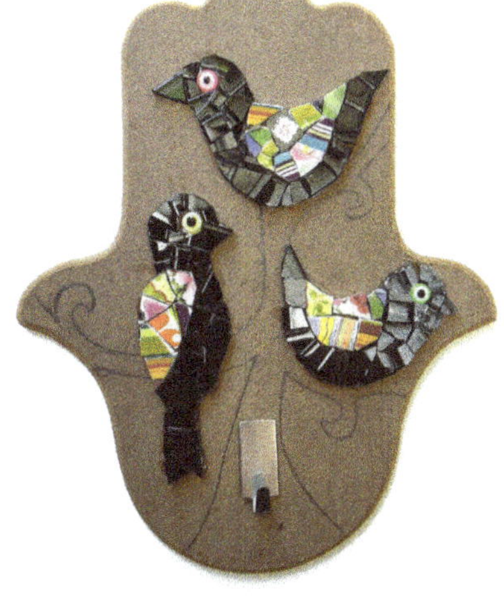

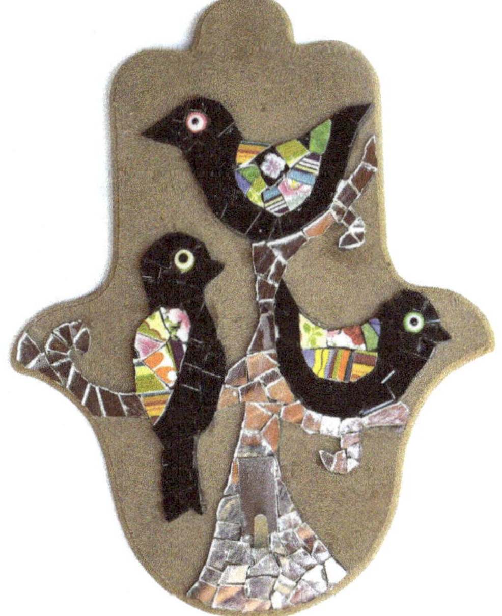

5 Cut a mirror into small shards and paste tightly on the trunk and branches.

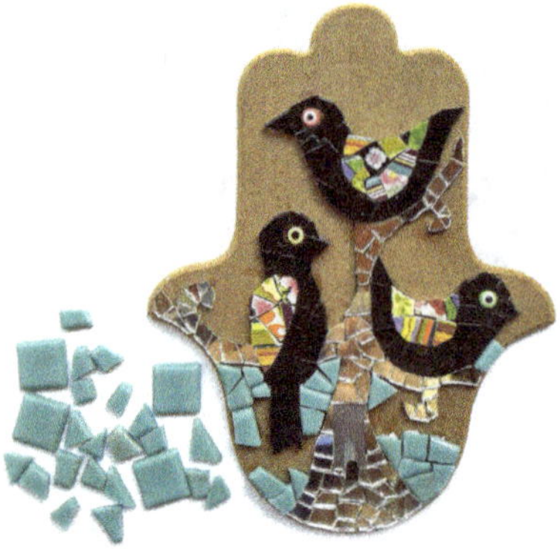

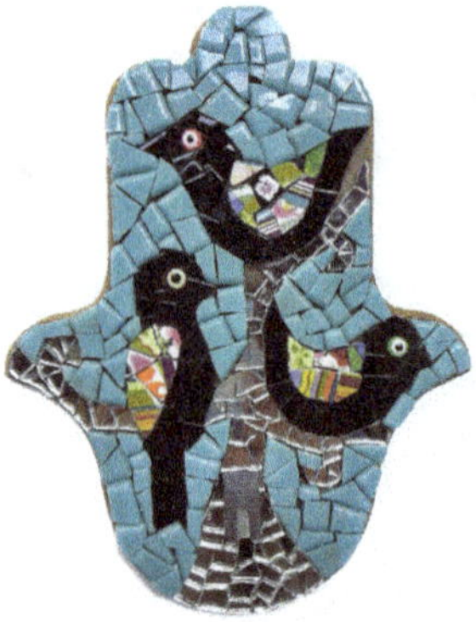

6 Cut turquoise ceramic or glass squares into small shards and fill in the background.

7 Prepare light gray grout according to manufacturer instructions, apply to the piece and clean thoroughly.

8 Once the grout is dry, you can glue a hanger to the back and put it up on a wall.

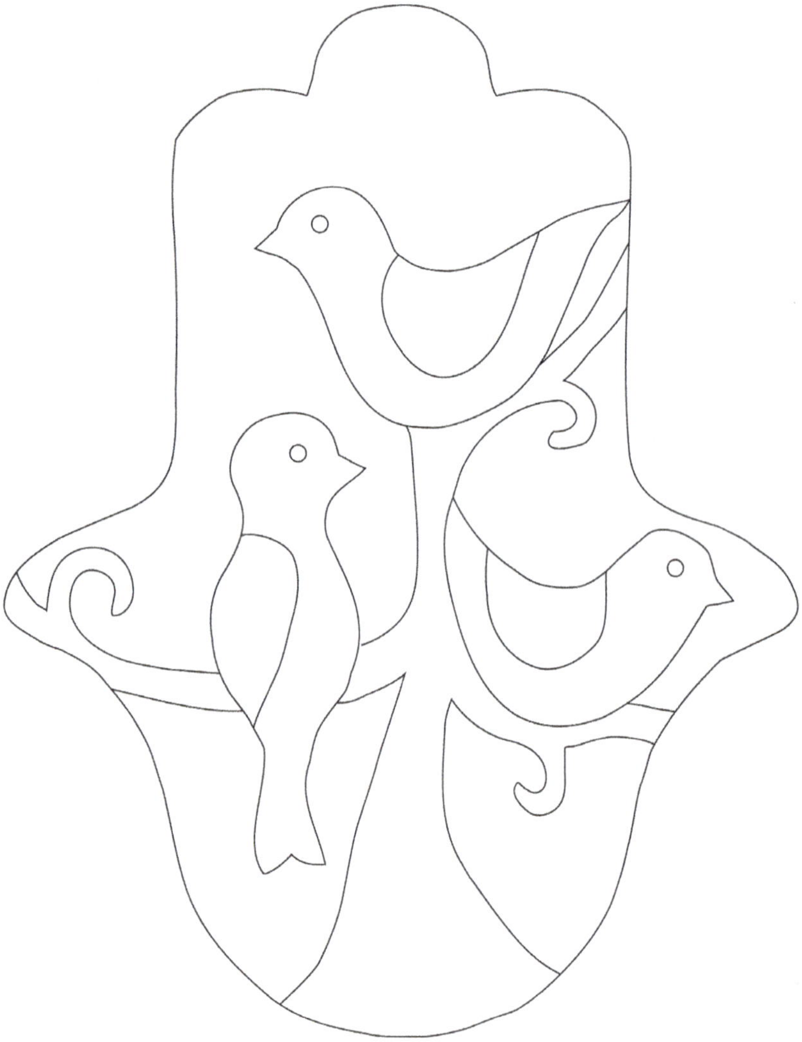

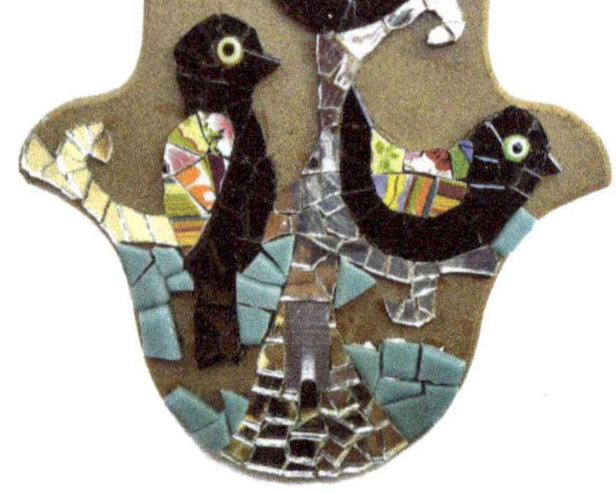

Pattern for the hamsa: Enlarge on a photocopier by 170% for a full size design

Tip: When pasting the background, you don't have to fill in an entire area in one go. You can apply glue to smaller areas and paste on each one before moving on to the next. By the time you'll reach them again they'll already be dry.

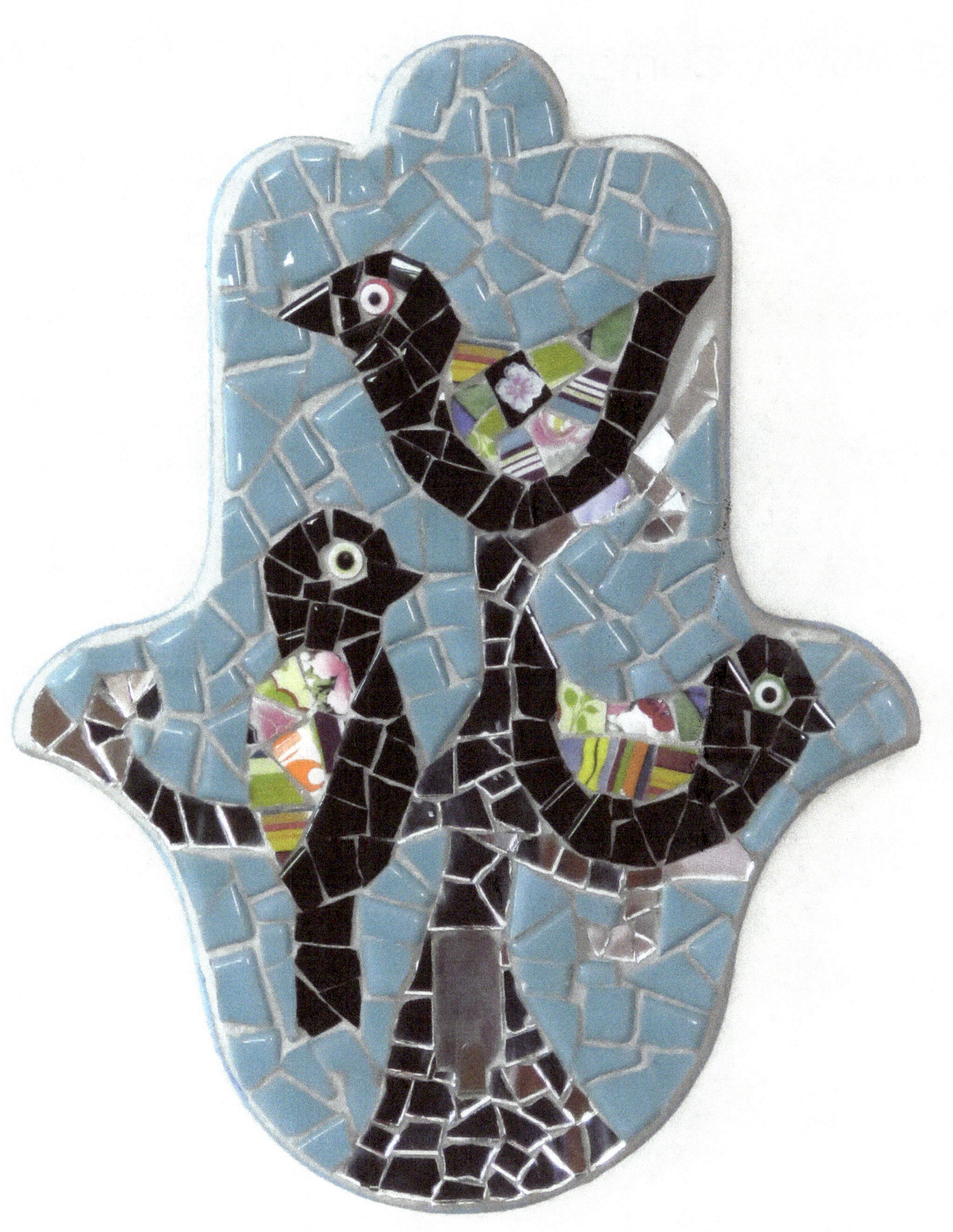

Combining Media

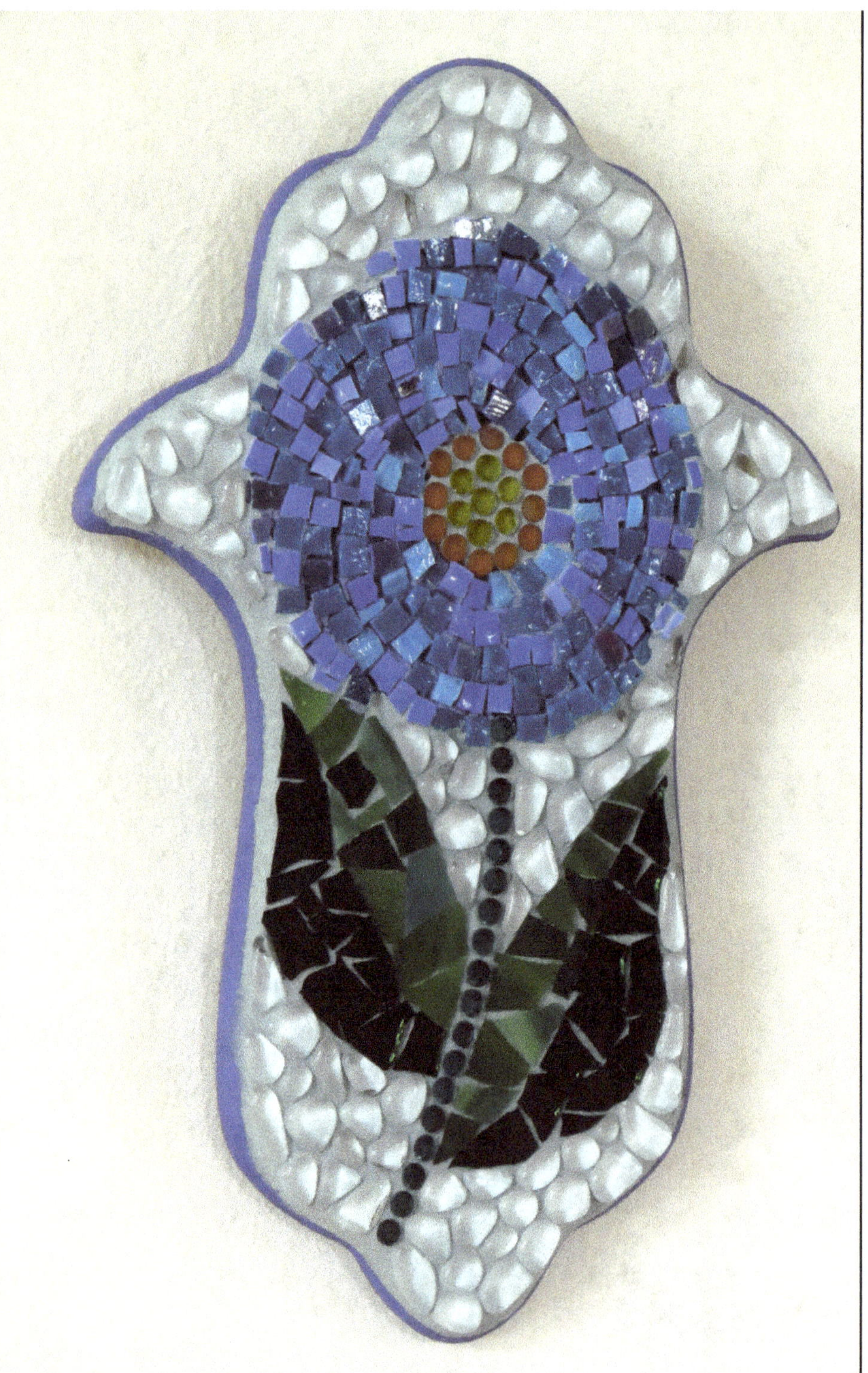

One of the things I like about mosaic is the ability to blend different colors and media in one piece while still maintaining harmony. Incorporating various media also makes the creation process more interesting, and the work itself richer and sometimes with a 3D effect.

In this hamsa, the blue flower is made of small shards of smalti glass in several different shades and heights. At its center are tiny glass circles, which compose the stem as well. The leaves are made of green glass in two shades, and the background is made of clear, rounded plastic drops. The blue flower is crafted without grout, while the rest is held together with gray grout.

At the center of this hamsa is azure glass with a special shape which I found lying around. I've also incorporated azure beads, different shades of glass and small polymer clay flowers. Here, it's important to consider the direction and shapes of the shards, to give off a feeling of flight. Note that each color is cut in a different manner.

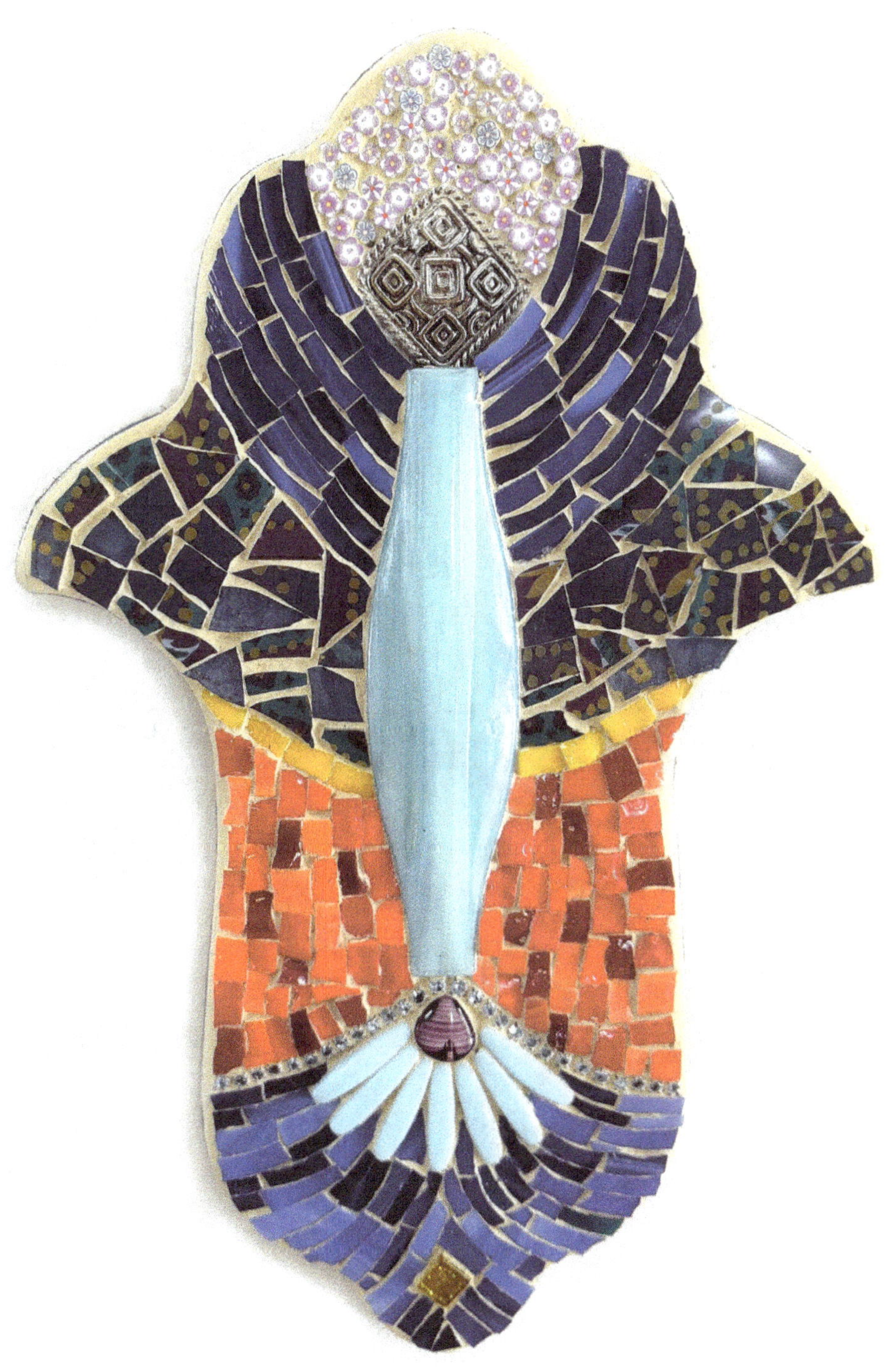

Colored Hamsas - Red, Green, Purple and Blue

Each hamsa is a different ball game, and I was in the mood to craft a series of small hamsas, each with its own different shades. I gathered up glasses, beads, squares and polymer clay flowers, sorted by color, and the results are thus: Four hamsas in shades of blue, purple, red and green, each with a different pattern according to the materials I chose. There is an infinite variety of materials you can use. Just try and see!

All four hamsas are pasted on a wooden board measuring 29x19cm / 11.4x7.5"

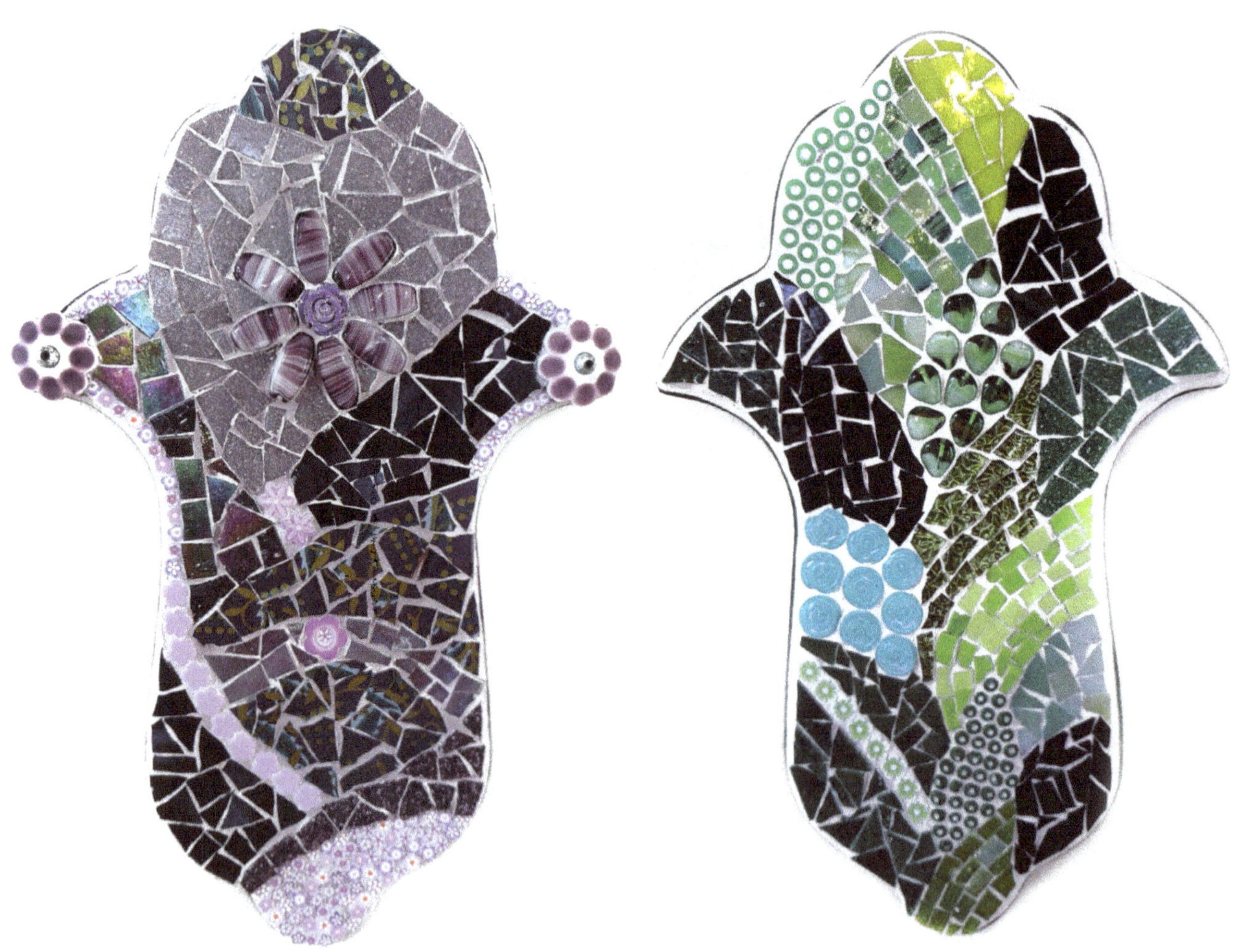

Purple hamsa: Purple glass, cut glass squares, tiny polymer clay flowers, decorated glass, glass beads and flower beads.

Green hamsa: 5 shades of green glass, glass beads, several sizes of round beads and polymer clay flowers.

Red hamsa: Glass in shades of red, colored glass, polymer clay flowers and several sizes of red beads.

Blue hamsa: Glass and glass tiles in shades of blue and azure, blue stone beads, tiny azure beads and golden beads for borders.

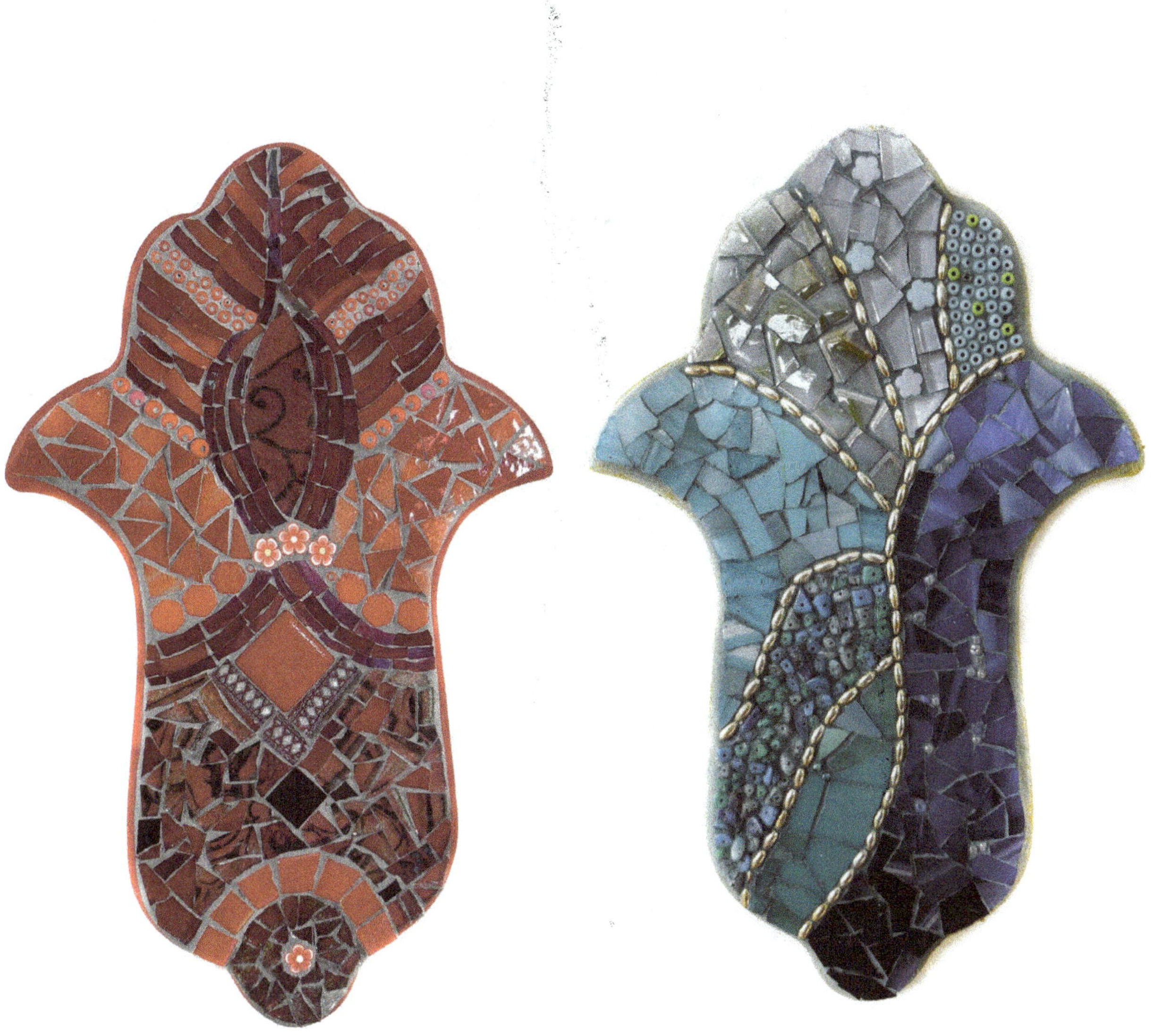

Bead Hamsas

I have a massive collection of beads. Some from necklaces taken apart, others purchased. Every necklace which has run its course ends up in the bead box. I also keep various jewelry parts from different materials, all of which end up in my mosaics.

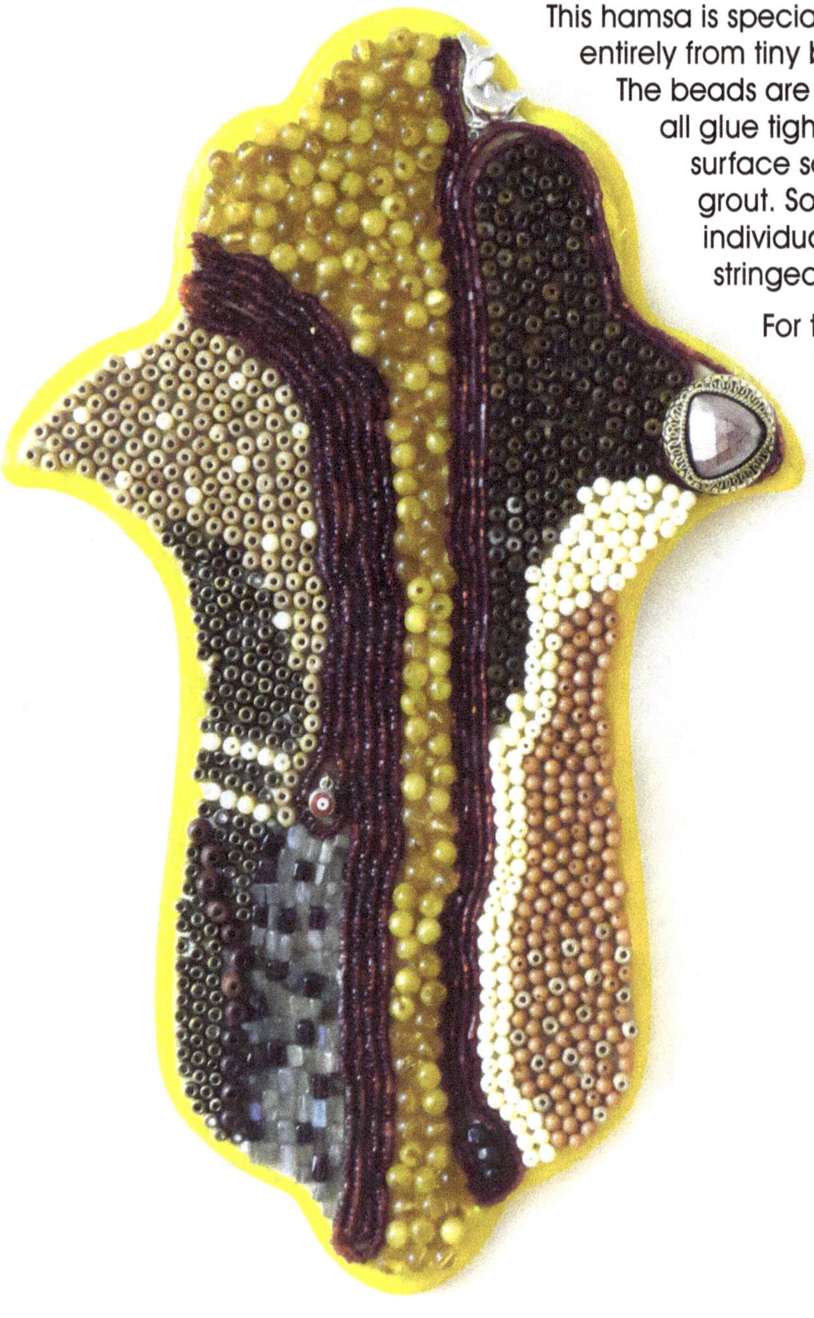

This hamsa is special since it's composed entirely from tiny beads in shades of brown. The beads are wood, metal and plastic, all glue tightly on a painted wood surface so there's no need for grout. Some beads are pasted individually, and some are still stringed together.

For this type of delicate work, it's recommended that you use tweezers and a strong plastic adhesive, so the beads don't come apart.

This is arduous work and is suitable mainly for small hamsas, but I find it quite enjoyable.

Students' Hamsas

Some of my students also fell in love with my passion for mosaic hamsas. Most of them craft small hamsas as gifts, but two of them, Dorit and Nava, created large hamsas that now hang on a wall at the entrance to their house.

The two hamsas were made onto a mesh using tile glue, and both include a bird motif, made of glass and mirrors.

In **Dorit's hamsa** (the left one), you can see a single bird. The contours are composed of cut mirrors, the interior of the hamsa is a combination of white and light pink glass, and the fingers are blue glass.

Nava's hamsa is a bit unusual shape. You can see a contour made from strips of cut glass. The hamsa itself features black decorations on droplet-shaped leaves (prefabricated elements) and a turquoise glass bird. The backdrop is crafted from several shades of white glass. Dark gray grout.

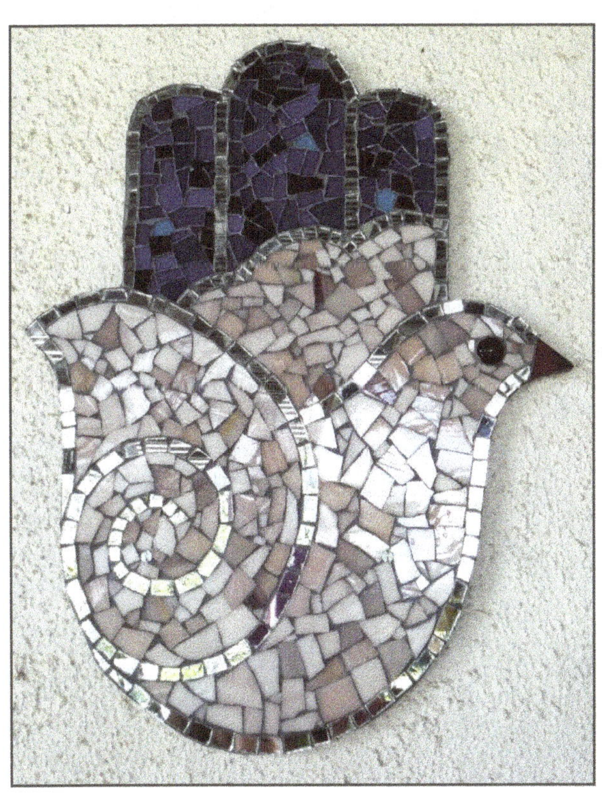

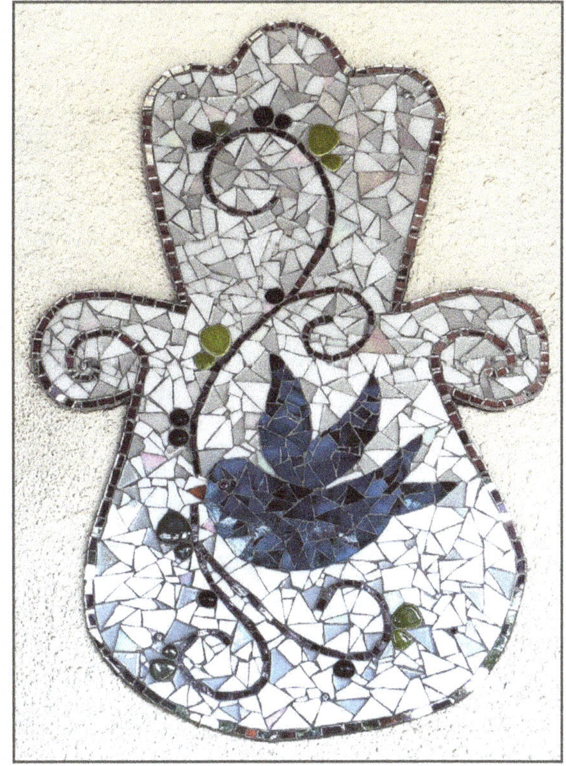

Hamsa for Peace

Mosaic artist Ariela Kedem came up with an idea, to which 50 more mosaic artists from all of Israel joined in: **A hamsa for peace**. A meeting of people from all walks of life, people from different fields and genders,to create one giant hamsa (1.2m tall), composed of small hamsas created by the participants.

One of the meeting's goals was to advance a social message of acceptance, tolerance and hope for peace.

The activity took place on a voluntary basis, inviting different sectors like Jews and Arabs, elderly and youth, at-risk teens, religious and secular people, trauma sufferers and others.

I had the honor and pleasure of participating in this blessed venture, and the hamsa you see below was created by youth and elderly people working together. I supplied them with cut meshes linked together to a hamsa pattern on cardboard, and they pasted with white glue, creating together with mixed media a variety of pieces, each by their ability, mainly with squares to ease the cutting.

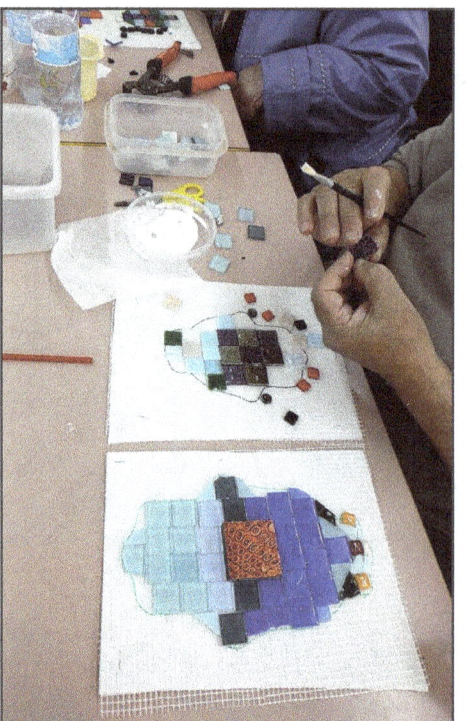

I cut out the finished hamsas and glued them onto the large one, and added a black background made of cut tiles.

The project succeeded far more than I anticipated. The hamsas traveled around for two years, each time growing in numbers and in increasingly impressive exhibitions. The message was loud and clear – in art, all are equal, there is no right or wrong, and the most important thing is the experience of creating together, which benefits everyone.

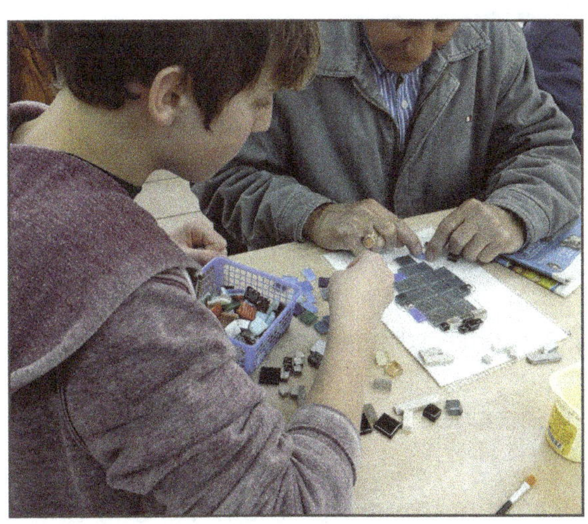

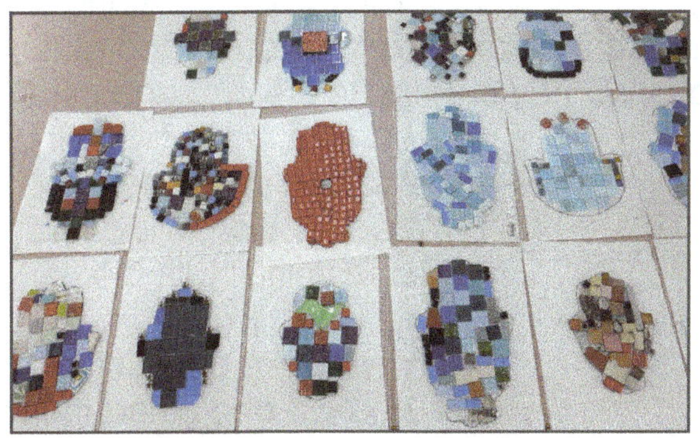

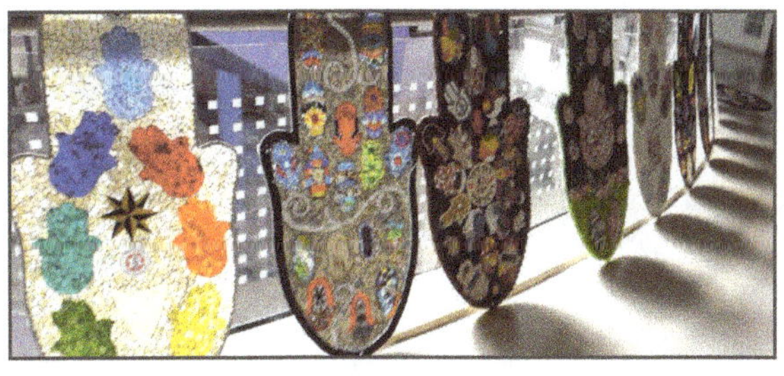

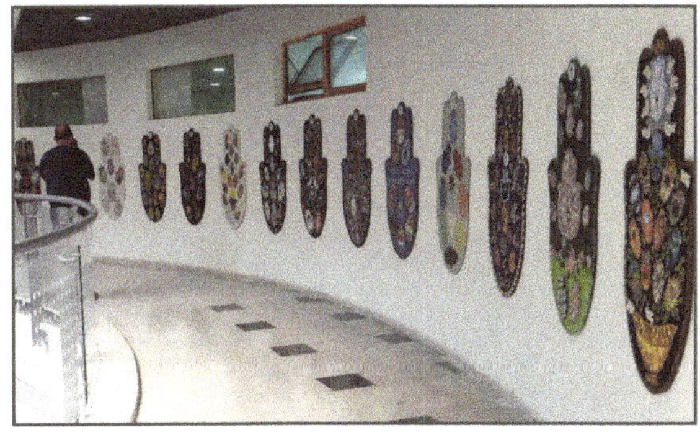

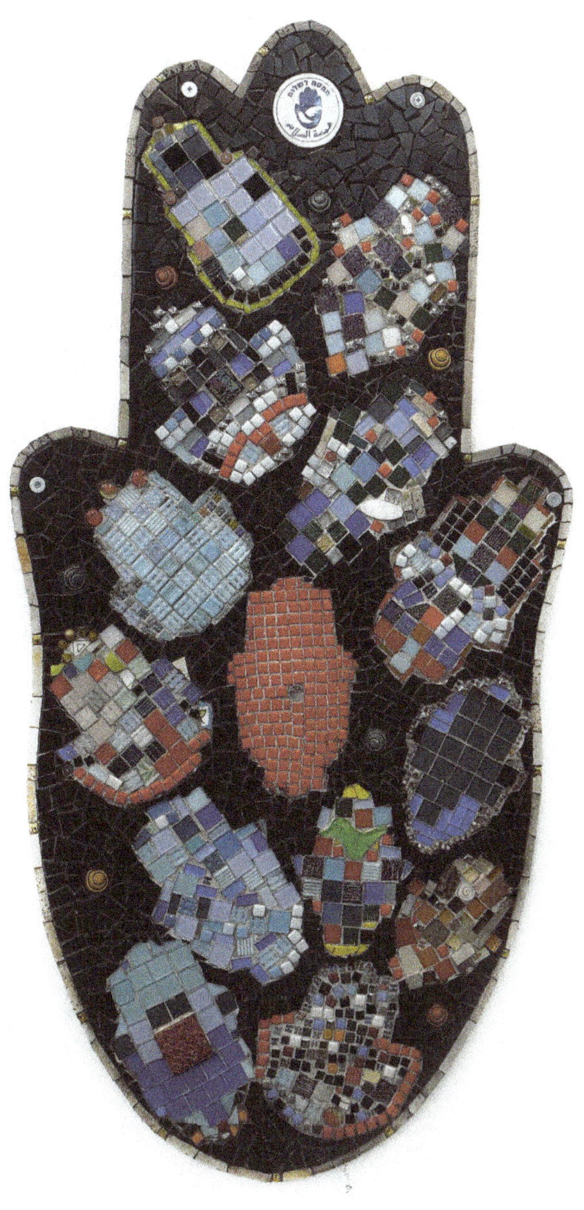

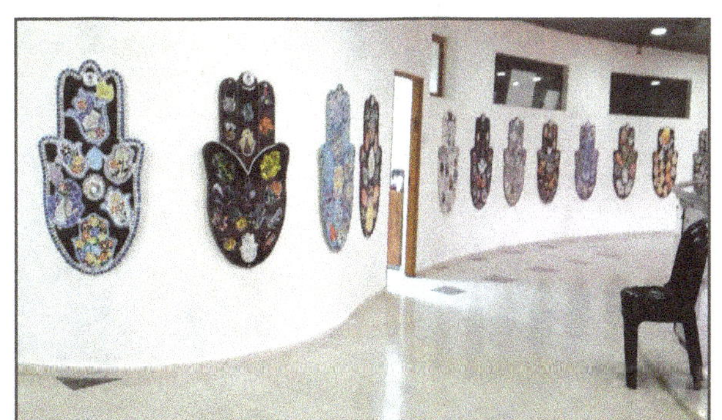

Communal Hamsas

A large mosaic project can make for a great collective experience, and can even promote important messages.

These hamsas were crafted by Jewish and Arab 9th graders, with the help of their teachers.

The idea was to hold several meetings where the students sat together, became acquainted and crafted together. These were two population groups who lived not far from one another, but knew nothing of each other's cultures.

Every student was paired up with a member of the other group and received a mesh with a painting of a hamsa on cardboard. Using a variety of materials, I provided (cut ceramic tiles, ceramic and glass square, and various decorations), they created interesting and unique hamsas, each by their own skill and patience. The cooperation was amazing and fruitful, with the teachers joining in. After drying, we cut out the hamsas and glued them together with tile glue to the school's entrance wall. The grout was applied after that, to each hamsa individually.

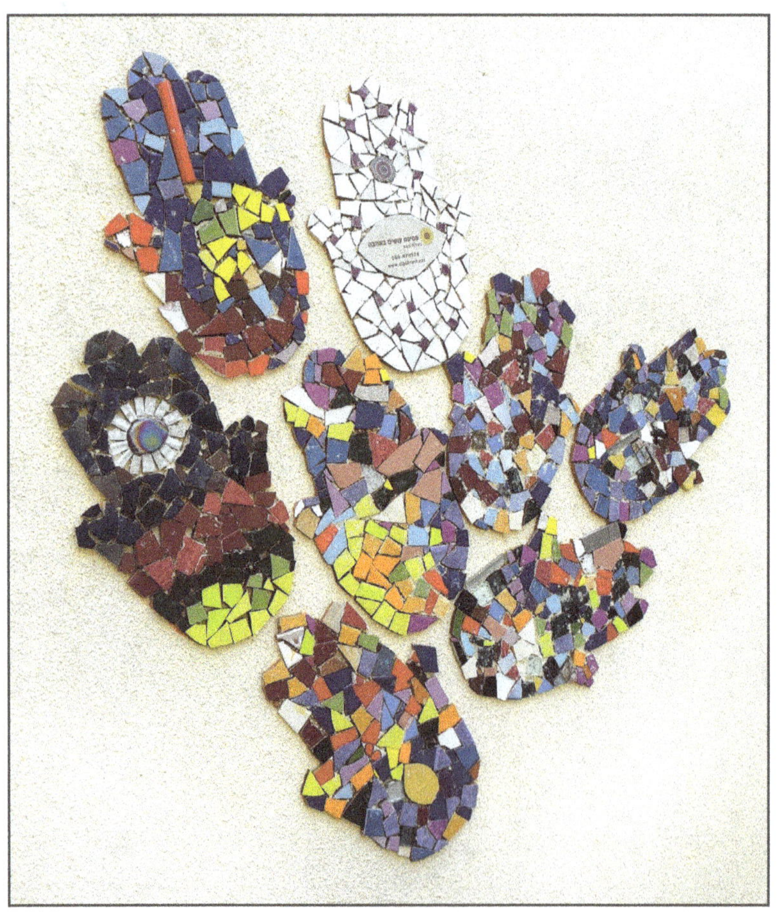

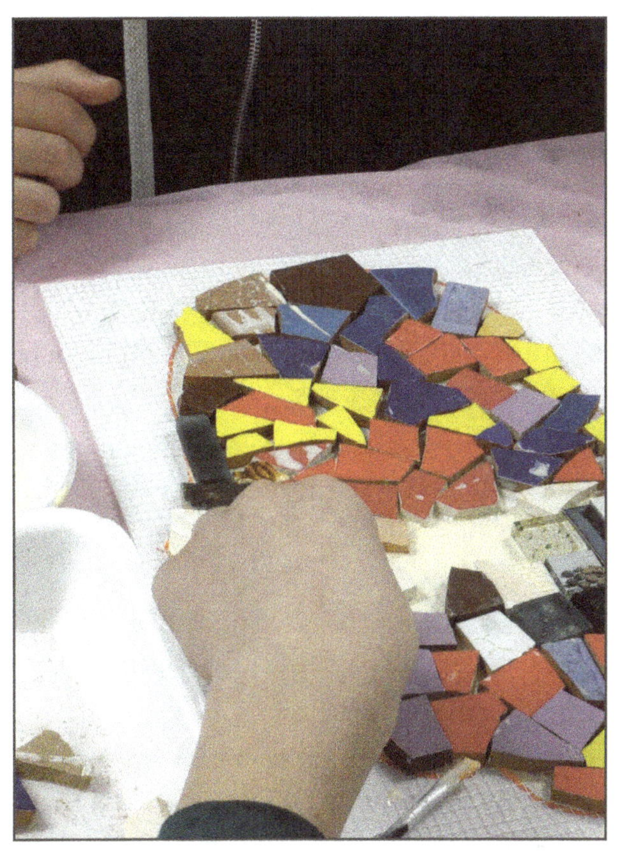 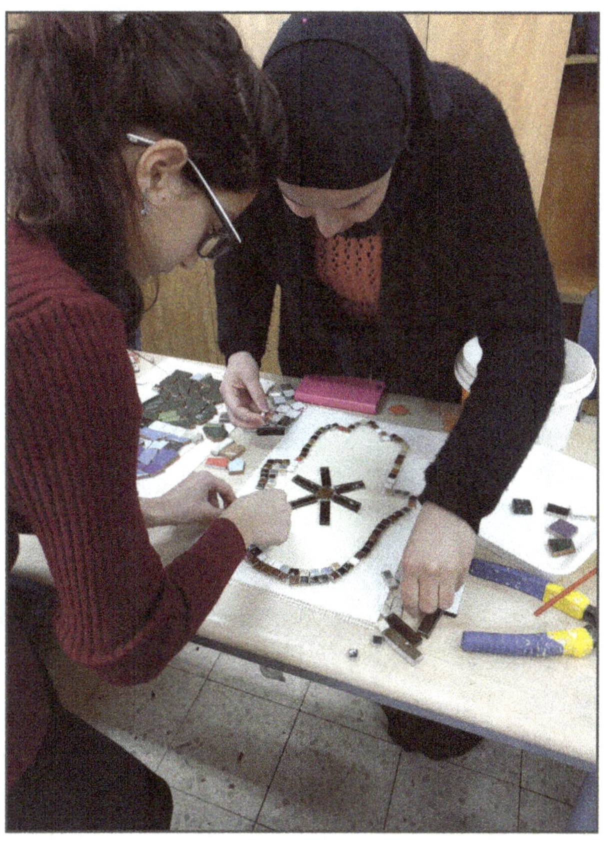

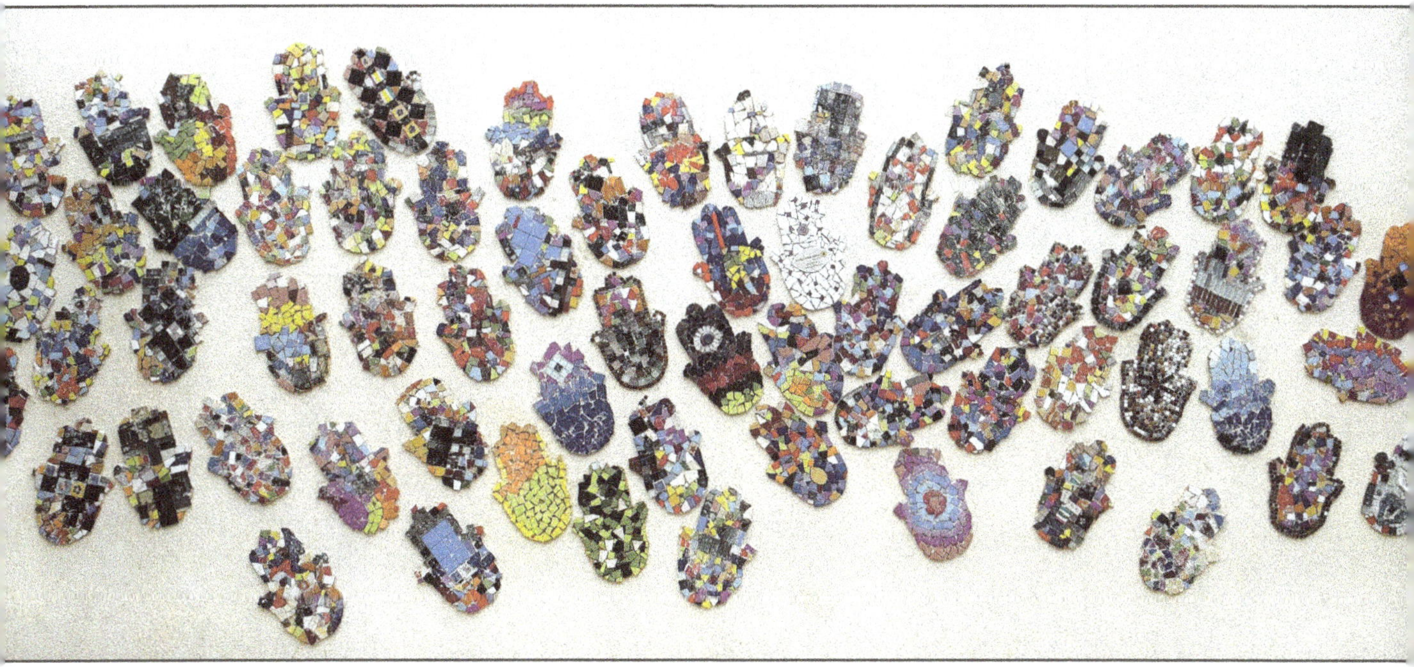

Summary

Over the years, I've created dozens of mosaic hamsas. I've discovered my penchant for this shape, which provides a challenge every time, and is also great as a small, lovely gift.

In this book, I've used the hamsa motif to teach various techniques, as well as media and glue combinations. All said techniques, ideas and motifs can be applied to other mosaics in your own original creations.

I hope that this book expanded your mind and knowledge, and taught you to look for unconventional media for your mosaics. I for one, discovered that bead shops are a great place for searching, and I mainly look for flat beads which are easy to glue.

I've tried to present you with a variety as wide as possible of cutting methods and how to match them to the media. Pay attention to the cut's influence on the nature of the piece, and plan your cuts in advance.

You can now print inscriptions as you wish and incorporate them in your mosaics. You can create poems, names, big captions and more – the technique you learned is simple, but can add another dimension to the mosaic.

And last but not least – Be safe. It's crucial that you wear gloves when working with glass or cleaning the mosaic, wear a mask or goggles when preparing the grout, and clean small debris with a brush. This way, you'll enjoy both the process and the finished product with no hiccups.

The designs in this book are original, and the patterns can be downloaded as PDFs to print at home.

Even if you aren't too big on spirituality, I believe every home can be made nicer with a lovely hamsa – At the very least, it can't hurt. Especially if it's hand-made.

Keep your spirit creative.

Yours,

Sigalit Eshet

There is a bonus for you. All the patterns that are showed in this book, are available in a pdf file, for your use:

Just type **http://bit.ly/38c2faB** in your browser and get it.

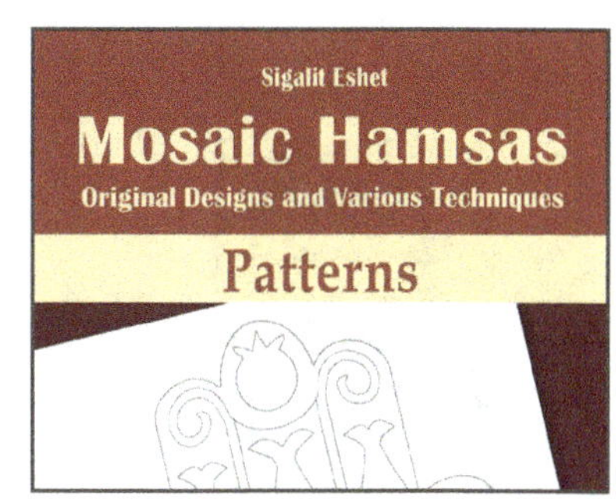

If from some reason you can't get the file, please email me and I will mail it to you:

Sigalit@sigalitart.net

If you loved this book, **Please leave a review on Amazon** and let other people enjoy making some mosaic hamsas.

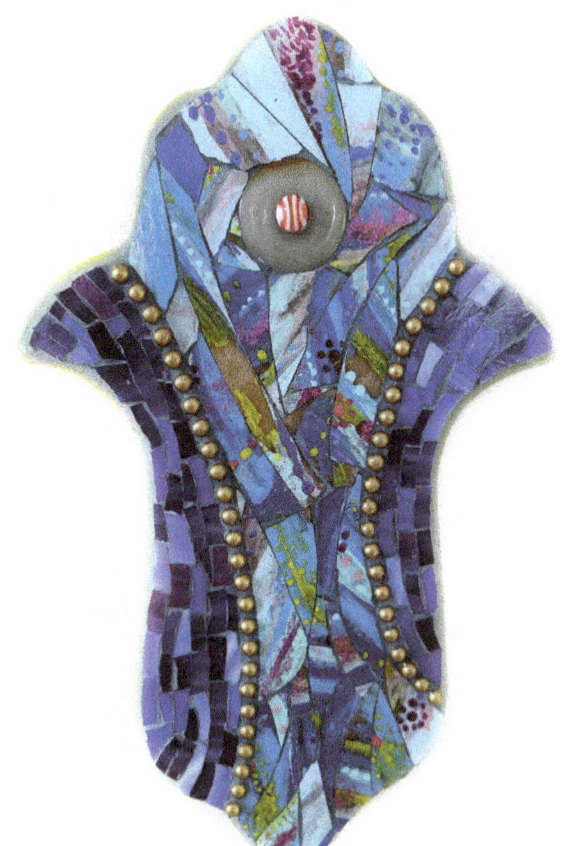

Other books on Amazon:

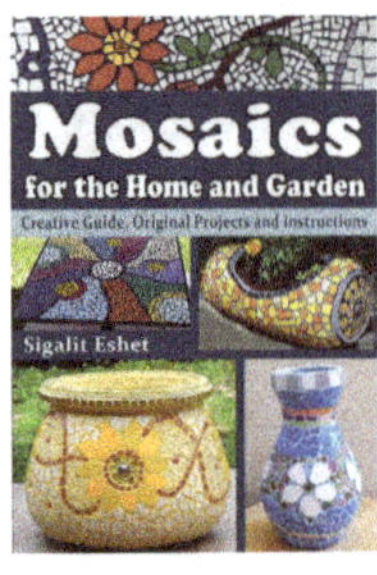

Mosaics for the Home and Garden

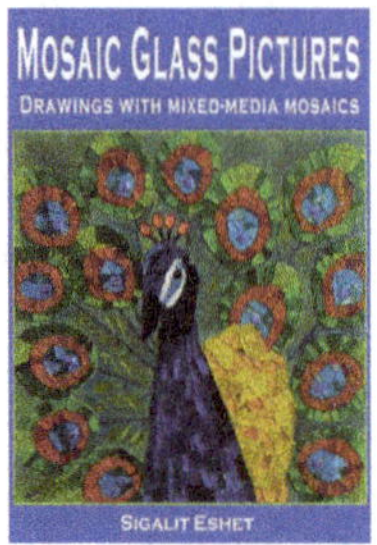

Mosaic Glass Pictures

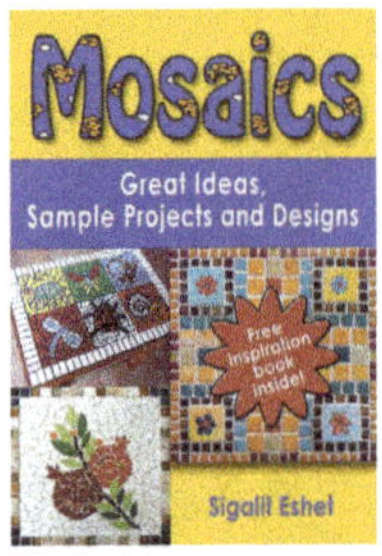

Mosaics: Great Ideas and Projects

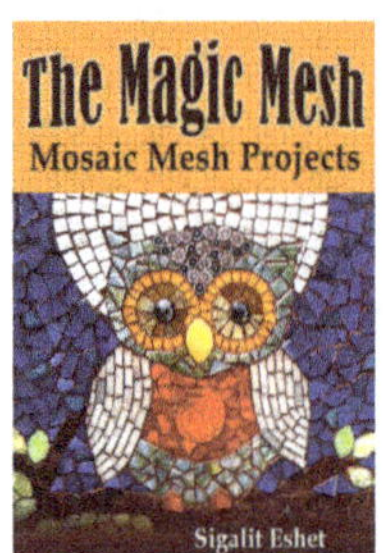

The Magic Mesh - Mosaic Mesh Projects

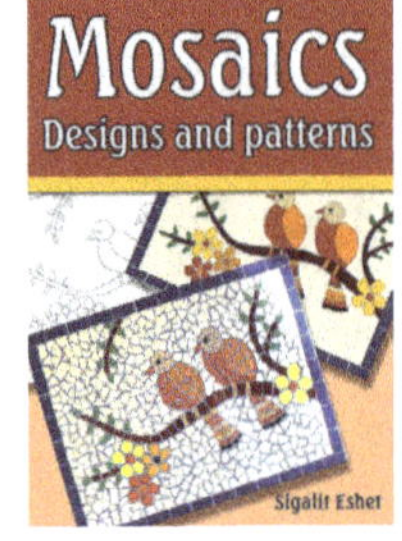

Mosaics - Designs and patterns

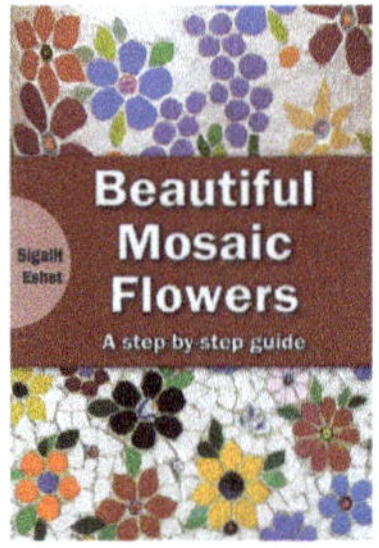

Beautiful Mosaic Flowers

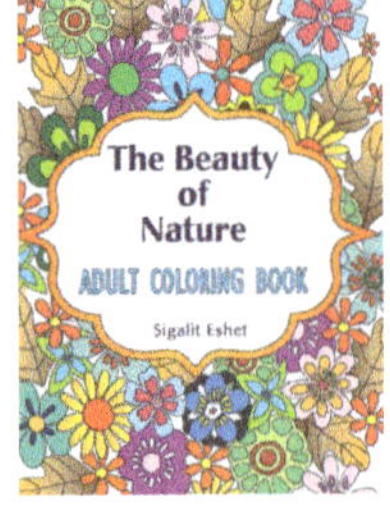

The beauty of nature: Adult coloring book

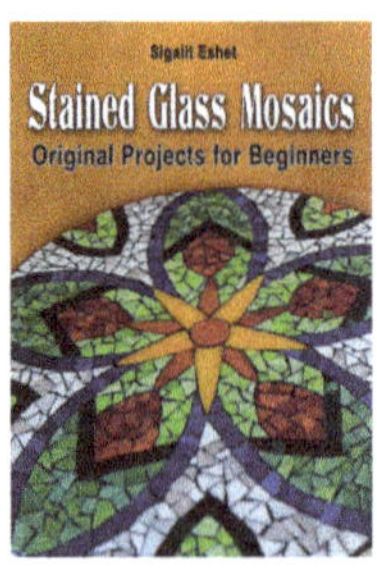

Stained Glass Mosaic

www.ingramcontent.com/pod-product-compliance
Lightning Source LLC
Chambersburg PA
CBHW081300130726
47998CB00010B/2877